He is the
STILL
POINT
of the
turning world

MARK LINK, S.J.

ARGUS COMMUNICATIONS
CHICAGO, 60657

CONTENTS

DESIGN BY GENE TARPEY

ACKNOWLEDGEMENTS
Scripture Quotations are from *Good News for Modern Man*—the New Testament in
Today's English Version—copyright American Bible Society 1966.

Psalms quotations are from *FIFTY PSALMS*—an attempt at a new translation by
Huub Oosterhuis et al—Published by Herder and Herder
232 Madison Avenue, New York 10016.

Teilhard de Chardin quotations are from *Hymn of the Universe*—Copyright 1961 by
Editions Du Seuil—Copyright © 1965 by Wm. Collins Sons & Co. Ltd., London and
Harper and Row Publishers, Inc., New York.

PHOTO CREDITS
Joe Benge 6,18,20,23,31,41,75,77,85,91,104—Greg Conners 19
William Crowley 24,69,70,109—Richard Dalle Molle 96—Don Doll 45,65,72,93
Art Dugan 9,48,63,89,116—Bob Fitch 12,13,17,113—Andy Fylypowycz 112
Gene Gasperini 97— Jack Glaser 4, 33
Algimantas Kezys 15,28,37,56,57,60,80,92 *top*, 100, 105
Gene Korba 40,46,47,64,66,/1,83,86,92 *bottom*, 94,102,108,114
Mark Link 26,74,88,106—Joseph Dwight 10,62,118—Jerome F. Riordan 67
St. Ignatius C.P. 61,73,99—Gene Tarpey 2,14,22,25,29,34,35,36,38,42,50,51,52,53,54,58,
59,68,78,79,90,98,110,117,119—Jan Wessels 11—Wide World 8—Jean Zilligen 21

Come away
to a land of
freedom

1

THE STILL POINT
IN THE
CHANGING WORLD

ONE MAN'S LIFE

Down
the
corridor
of
time
has
travelled
a
man
whose
life
and
spirit
have
changed
men's
lives
and
shaped
the
course
of
history
as
no
other
man
has
ever
done.

THE STILL POINT

Art galleries capture his life in paintings
libraries are lined with books
exploring his thought.
Hospitals and schools
are dedicated to his memory.

He is the focus of controversy,
the rallying point of unity,
the object of love,
the subject of debate,
a basis for hope,
and the goal of lives.
No man interested in
the meaning of life
and its ultimate questions
can ignore him.

He towers above
the giants of history.
To some he is an uneasy feeling
in times of silence;
to others he is a sunrise of hope
in a night of darkness.
To all he is a challenge.

PARADOX

Reflecting on
Jesus' presence in history,
the poet, Crashaw
was stirred to write:

Welcome all wonders in one sight!
Eternity shut in a span!
Summer in Winter, Day in Night!
Heaven in earth, and God in man!

I WONDER

I often wonder
whether Jesus was
a man
of flesh and blood like ourselves,
or a thought
without a body . . .
or an idea
that visits the vision of man.
Jesus The Son of God
Kahlil Gibran
Published by Alfred A. Knopf, Inc.

A MATTER OF HISTORY

One of the earliest references to Jesus,
in nonreligious history,
is found in the writings
of the Roman historian,
Tacitus (37-100AD).

The reference occurs
in the context of a great fire
that gutted the city of Rome.
Rumors circulated that the emperor,
Nero,
had a hand in it.

To squelch the rumors,
a scapegoat had to be found.
Nero found it in a group of "culprits"
called "Christians."

In his history of Roman emperors,
Tacitus wrote:

"Therefore, in order to disprove the rumor . . .
Nero falsely accused culprits
and subjected to most unusual punishment . . .
those whom the populace called Christians.
The author of this name,
Christ,
was put to death
by the procurator Pontius Pilate,
while Tiberius was emperor."
Annales 15. 44:2-3

WHERE DO WE GO FROM HERE?

Until recently,
Russian officials have tried
to convince their public
that Jesus was a mere myth,
a legendary figure.
As late as 1964,
this position was argued in popular writings,
such as Nikonendo's
"The Legend of Jesus."

This view is now challenged
by competent Russian historians.
Writing in *Science and Religion*,
the Soviet's leading atheistic journal,
the historian, Nevgod, argues:

if the parables
and vivid images of the Gospel
were created to make Jesus real
and acceptable,
one would have to conclude
that the biblical writers
were sheer geniuses.

The words and sermons of Jesus
are so striking
and vivid
that they clearly reflect
a living oral speech pattern.

Sayings, like the coin of Caesar
and the Sabbath being made for man
were made off the cuff
during a hot debate.
They impressed hearers
and were quickly passed on
from mouth to mouth.

Nevgod concludes
by asking the key question:
Now that we admit that
Jesus is real,
where do we go from here?

WHO DO YOU SAY I AM?

It is not uncommon to hear someone say,
"Christians claim God is like this.
Jews say he is like that.
Moslems say something else!
I'm so mixed up,
I don't know what to think
or who to believe."

One is reminded
of the four blind men
who went to the circus.
The question arose,
"What does an elephant look like?"
One blind man felt the elephant's leg
and said he looked like a tree trunk.
Another felt his tail
and said he looked like a rope.
The third felt his tusk
and said he looked like a sword.
The last man
felt his side
and said he looked like a wall.

Which of the blind men was right?

Perhaps the best answer
is to say that each one
was right —
from his own viewpoint.
But each blind man
was not completely right.
Only by dialoging together
could they get a complete
and more accurate view
of what an elephant is like.

In a sense,
this is the way it is with God.

The question arises:
How can any one religious group
claim to be closer to the truth
about God
than any other.
For example,
by what right can a Christian
claim to have a privileged insight
into what God is like?

The answer rests
on the Christian's faith
in Jesus.
Jesus claimed to know God
as no other man knew him.
Jesus did more.
He claimed identity with God.
He said to Phillip,
"Whosoever has seen me
has seen the Father . . .
I am in the Father
and the Father is in me."
John 14:9

No man in history
ever claimed what Jesus claimed.
Mohammed acknowledged himself to be a sinner.
Buddha rejected personal veneration.
No religious leader
identified himself with God
in the manner that Jesus did.
If Jesus was who he claimed to be,
then Christians can correctly claim
access to a personally revealed knowledge of God.

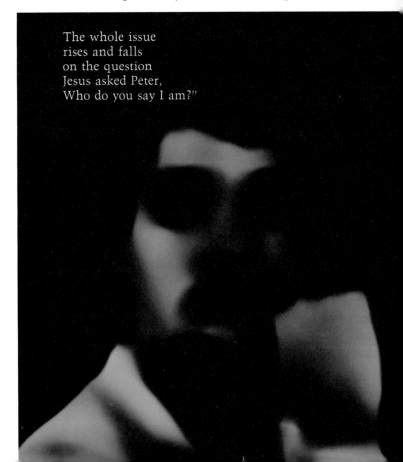

The whole issue
rises and falls
on the question
Jesus asked Peter,
Who do you say I am?"

ALWAYS THERE

After 19 centuries he is there.
We cannot get him
out of our minds
and out of our lives.
Always he is there,
and we must do something
about him.

What think ye of Christ?
We have to think something of him
What shall I do then with Jesus?
We have to do something with him.
For we cannot ignore him.

Sermon Reader's Digest
Heltzel

PRIMITIVE

". . . what primitive mythology it is,
that a divine Being should become incarnate,
and atone for the sins of men
through his blood."

Rudolf Bultmann

MORE THAN MAN?

GENERAL BERTRAND

"I cannot conceive . . .
how a great man like you
can believe that the Supreme Being
ever exhibited himself to men
under a human form,
with a body, a face,
mouth, and eyes.
Let Jesus be whatever you please—
the highest intelligence,
the purest heart . . .
the most singular being
who ever existed—
I grant it.
Still he was simply a man . . ."

NAPOLEON

"I know men,
and I tell you that Jesus is not a man . . .
You speak of Caesar,
of Alexander,
of their conquests,
and of the enthusiasm
they enkindled in the hearts of their soldiers;
but can you conceive
of a dead man making conquests

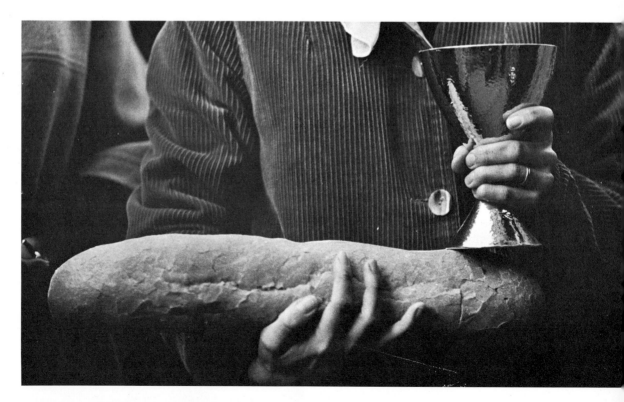

with an army faithful
and entirely devoted
to his memory?
My armies have forgotten me,
even while living,
as the Carthaginian army forgot Hannibal.
Such is our power!
A single battle lost crushes us,
and adversity scatters our friends . . .

"I have so inspired multitudes
that they would die for me . . .
the lightning of my eye,
my voice,
a word from me,
then the sacred fire
was kindled in their hearts.
I do, indeed,
possess the secret
of this magical power,
which lifts the soul
but I could never impart it
to anyone.
None of my generals
ever learned it from me;
nor have I
the means of perpetuating
my name and love for me
in the hearts of men.

"Now that I am at St. Helena,
now that I am alone . . .
who fights and wins for me?"

The History of Napoleon Bonaparte Vol. II
J. S. Abbot

DOES IT REALLY MATTER?

"Is that Thomas back?"

"No, Lord, it's a group of students."

"And?"

"They've signed a petition.
It says they love you,
no matter whose son you are.
They love your gentleness and
tolerance and humility.
They want you to know that they
don't care if you're God or not . . ."

Jesus Christs
A. J. Langguth

MODERN CHRISTIANS?

In his novel, *Studs Lonigan,*
James T. Farrell has Davey Cohen,
a Jew,
stop into a Greek restaurant
for a cup of coffee.
There Davey
gets into a discussion with Christy,
the waiter,
and another guy,
named Pete.

"And in Los Angeles,
they have fanatics.
Christians,"
said Christy.

"Sure.
All kinds of bugs.
There's more fake saviors there
than any place in the world."

"Christians,
Love your neighbor as yourself.
Christians," sneered Pete.

"And what the hell did they do
to get their God
but steal him from the Jews,"
laughed Davey . . .

"Jesus, he was great. . . .
Christians,
they drag him in the mud.
They don't love Jesus,
or follow his example.
They are afraid.
They have a God of fear.
That's religion . . . fear."

"The Irish
made a shanty Irishman
out of Christ,"
Davey said.

"Yes, Jesus was a noble man.
The Christians . . .
they put him
in a sink of superstition."

"Yeah, Christy," said Davey,
kind of agreeing with him,
feeling that agreement got him even
with Irish bastards
like Lonigan . . .

EARLY CHRISTIANS

Pliny the Younger (62-113AD),
was a Roman governor in Asia Minor.
His reign was checkered with unrest.
In a letter of explanation
to the Emperor Trajan,
he places much of the blame
on a group of people called "Christians."
He wrote:

The method I have observed
towards those who have been brought before me
as Christians
is this:
I asked them
whether they were Christians;
if they admitted it,
I repeated the question twice,
and threatened them with punishment;
if they persisted,
I ordered them
to be at once punished . . .

Some among those who were accused
denied it,
the rest owned indeed
that they had been . . .
but had now renounced that error.
They all worshipped your statue
and the images of the gods,
uttering imprecations
at the same time
against the name Christ.
They affirmed . . .
that they met on a stated day
before it was light,
and addressed a form of prayer
to Christ,
as to a divinity,
binding themselves by a solemn oath,
not for the purposes of wicked design,
but never to commit any fraud,
theft, or adultery,
never to falsify their word,
nor deny a trust
when they should be called upon
to deliver it up;

after which it was their custom
to separate,
and then reassemble,
to eat in common a harmless meal . . .
I deemed it expedient, therefore,
to adjourn all further proceedings,
in order to consult you. . . .
In fact, this contagious superstition
is not confined to the cities only,
but has spread its infection
among the neighboring villages
and country.
Nevertheless,
it still seems possible
to restrain its progress.

Letters, Book 10, Letter 97

WHO'S TO BLAME?

Harvey Cox asks this question:
"Who is responsible for ruining Christmas?"
Most people have an instant pop-up answer:
commercialization.
Cox disagrees.
He admits the hucksters
have had a hand in it.
But the main blame
falls to many so-called
followers of Christ.

Cox says we have
"distorted and diluted
the story of Jesus."
He maintains that
the very fact that Christianity has survived
is something of a miracle.
Only the persistent power of Jesus'
personality has kept Christianity alive.

Cox says Christians have distorted
and diluted
the story of Jesus
in three ways.
Whether you agree with him entirely
or not,
his ideas are insightful
and instructive.

First, Cox says,
we have made the story of Jesus
over into a "life-denying philosophy."
Expanding on this idea, he says:

On at least two occasions,
the Gospels report that his enemies
rejected Jesus
because he had no interest in fasting
and was a "glutton and a winebibber." . . .

I wonder who drew those countless pictures
distributed by churches and Sunday schools
of a pale, effete Jesus?
Those pictures
have done more to destroy Jesus
than 100 of Herod's legions.

Second,
Cox maintains that we have tended
to turn Christianity into a "petty rule system."
We have distorted the image of Jesus
by picturing him
to be a "finicky" moralizer
who spent his life telling people
what *not* to do.
Commenting on this point,
Cox says:

Jesus came into a world
in some ways like ours,
where for most people,
religion had been reduced
to a set of rigid rules to worry about
and a bag of ritual flip-flops
to break open
when you transgressed them . . .

Jesus himself
spent his life breaking most of those taboos—
violating the Sabbath,
rapping with "impure" men and women . . .
When people did come to him
with moral dilemmas,
he invariably tossed the questions back at them
at a deeper level.
Whether he was confronted
by what some considered to be theft,
adultery,
tax evasion or whatever,
he consistently refused
to play the rulebook game.

Excerpted from "For Christ's Sake" by Harvey Cox.
Originally appeared in PLAYBOY magazine;
copyright 1969 by HMH Publishing Co. Inc.

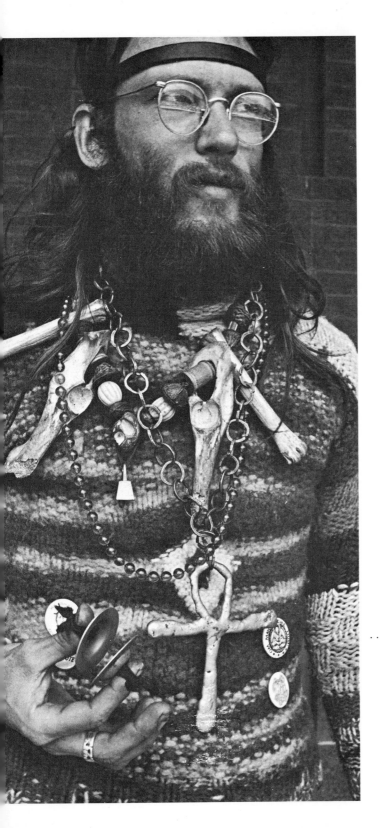

That is just what riled so many people.
He made them look within
and decide for themselves.
And that's scary.

This is not to say
that Jesus
had no interest in the great ethical issues of life.
He certainly did.
But there is a difference
between genuine morality
and petty moralism.
Jesus was concerned
about the folly
of looking for real satisfaction
in obsessively accumulating wealth.
He fought ethnic hatred,
religious snobbery,
intellectual pretense
and every form of cultural hauteur.
But a purveyor of rules
he was not . . .

. . . Most people
don't like to assume the responsibility
of making ethical decisions
for themselves.
They long desperately
for someone,
anyone,
to do it for them:
a shrink,
a professor,
Ann Landers.
Jesus refused.

scorned those in power
and defied imperial authority.
He cast his lot with the outs,
the riffraff and the misfits,
the Palestinian equivalent of hippies,
street people and untouchables.
He died the death
reserved for those found guilty of insurrection.
On the whole,
an unlikely candidate
for the Union League Club.

Cox ends his article saying:

I used to believe,
and even hope,
that mankind might someday outgrow
its religious phase
and live maturely
in the calm, cool light of reason.
But people have been predicting
the end of religion and the death of God
for centuries.
And I
no longer seriously believe it will happen,
nor do I hope it will.

Why?

First, because, with a few exceptions,
I am not very impressed
with the level of imagination,
compassion
or human vitality
of the people I know
who claim they have left religion behind. . . .

Second,
just as we have gotten comfortable with the idea
that religion was disappearing—
on the campuses, for example—
it came back in a swirl of swamis,
gurus, chants . . .
The incense business was never better. . . .
Whatever it is,
it suggests to me
that man is more essentially religious
than many of us have assumed.
He thirsts for mystery,
meaning,
community
and even some sort of ritual.

Third,
Cox says we have distorted and diluted
the character of Jesus
by "deradicalizing" him.
Touching on this point,
Cox says:

No imperial power
wastes nails,
boards and soldiers' time
crucifying contemplatives
or harmless spiritual mystics.
Jesus was neither . . .
The song Jesus' mother sings
after she conceives him
calls for
"casting down the mighty
from their thrones"
and "sending the rich away empty."
Jesus himself
announced that his mission
was one of liberating the captives.
He lampooned the rich,

LOSERS

The Gospel
is a much more powerful weapon
than our Marxist view of the world.

Yet it is we
who shall conquer you
in the end . . .

How can anyone believe
in the all-surpassing value
of this Gospel

if you do not practice it,
if you do not spread it,
if you sacrifice neither
your time
nor your money
for that purpose?

But you,
you are afraid of
soiling your hands.

Paix et Liberte

SHERIFF/SCOUT

When I hear someone say
that he rejects the Church,
Christ,
or Christianity,
I feel like saying,
"So would I,
if I had the same idea of them
that you probably have."
I find myself wishing
that they had never heard of the Church,
Christ, or Christianity.
Because the idea they have
of these
is often distorted.
Unfortunately,
it is not always their fault.

Wes Seeliger
expressed in parable form,
"what Christianity *really* is"
compared to
what "many people *think* it is."
He called the one view
pioneer theology;
the other view *settler* theology.
What follows
is a summary of some of his ideas.

The Church

In Settler theology
the church is a courthouse.
The old stone structure
dominates the town square.
Inside its walls
records are kept,
taxes are paid,
and trials are held for bad guys.
It is a symbol of security,
law, and order.

In Pioneer theology
the church is a covered wagon.
It is a house on wheels—
always on the move.
It bears the marks of life.
It creaks,
is scarred with arrow marks,
and bandaged with bailing wire.
The covered wagon
is always where the action is.

God

In settler theology
God is like a mayor.
He smokes big cigars
and lounges comfortably
in an overstuffed chair
in the courthouse office.
No one dares approach him.
Guys in black hats fear him.
Guys in white hats rely on him
to keep things under control.

In pioneer theology
God is like a trail boss.
He is rough and rugged—full of life.
He lives and fights with his men.
Without him the pioneers
would become fat and lazy.
He often gets down in the mud
with the pioneers to help
push the wagon
when it gets bogged down.

Jesus

In settler theology
Jesus is the sheriff.
He is the guy sent by the mayor
to enforce the rules.
He wears a white hat and
always outdraws the bad guys.
He also decides who
gets thrown into jail.

In pioneer theology
Jesus is a scout.
He rides out ahead to find out
which way the pioneers should go.
He lives all the dangers of the trail.
He doesn't ask the pioneers
to do what he didn't do first.
His spirit and guts
serve as a model to all.

Christian

In settler theology
the Christian is the settler.
His concern is
to stay out of the sheriff's way.
He tends a small garden.
His motto is "Safety First."
To him the courthouse is
a symbol of security,
order, and happiness.

In pioneer theology
the Christian is a pioneer.
He is a man of risk and daring,
hungry for adventure, new life.
He is tough, rides hard, and
knows how to handle himself
through trials and danger.
He enjoys the challenge of the trail.
He dies with his boots on.

Faith

In settler theology
faith is trusting in
the safety of the town,
obeying the laws,
believing the mayor
is always in the courthouse,
and keeping your nose clean.

In pioneer theology
faith is
the spirit of adventure.
It is the readiness
to move out,
to risk everything on the trail.

Sin

In settler theology
sin is
breaking one of
the town's ordinances.

In pioneer theology
sin is
wanting to turn back.

THE MAGNIFICENT TRUTH

The magnificent truth—
for each of us
who really cares to find out—
is that the Person
who masterminded all creation
was once
breathing, sleeping and eating
on this planet Earth
just as you and I are . . .

Reach Out
Tyndale House Publishers

FOR ALL NATIONS

"I have been studying your religion,"
the Japanese professor said,
"and I am convinced
that its philosophy of life
could bring lasting peace
to all nations.
But you have not fulfilled
the command of . . .
Jesus Christ.
He said to bring his teaching,
his Gospel,
to all men of all nations.
You . . . have not done this.
And you are not even making
a serious attempt to do it now.

"Take my country, for instance . . .
you who preach that you are interested
in all men
have only a few hundred priests here.
There is need for thousands. . . .

"I am afraid it is too late . . .
But I blame you
because you . . .
had the truth and yet you made
little more than a gesture to
bring it to our . . . people.

"I feel you have cheated us. . . .
But I hope you will not make
the same mistake again
in any other part of the world."

The Priest and a World Vision
James Keller

UNIQUE

I have read the four Gospels
several times
and . . . the Psalms twice,
and I feel that nothing
in our Confucian classics
is comparable to
the religious and moral doctrines
contained therein.

General Yang Tsin quoted in
Beyond East and West
C. H. Wu

LOVE DOES SUCH THINGS

Christianity holds
that the infinite God,
in the person of Jesus,
at a point in time,
crossed an unimaginable borderline
and personally entered history.

Before
such an undreamable dream
the intellect falters.
It was at this point
that a friend gave me a clue
that helped my understanding
more than any measure
of bare reason.
He said:
"But love does such things."

WE TEND TO BECOME...

There is a law of love that says:
we tend to become
like that which we love.

This law explains *why*
God became man.
It also explains
how we can become
like Christ.

People today
want a star to follow,
an ideal,
something to "hitch their wagons to"—
yes, a star.

ONLY IN ALONENESS

Presently
Jesus began to speak with us. . . .
And he told us
stories and parables,
and his voice enchanted us
so that we gazed upon him
as if seeing visions
and we forgot the cup and plate.

And I listened to him
as if I were in a land
distant and unknown. . . .

Nay, Jesus was not a phantom,
nor a conception of poets.
He was a man like
yourself and myself.

He saw visions we did not see, .
and heard voices we
did not hear . . .
He was upon earth
yet he was of the sky.
And only in our aloneness
may we visit the land
of his aloneness.

Jesus The Son of God
Kahlil Gibran
Published by Alfred A. Knopf, Inc.

2

THE REFERENCE POINT OF
OF
HUMAN HISTORY

NIGHT TRAVELLER

Man: I travel
an unknown land
to an unknown city.
The road is dark and misty.
Soaring mountains
and roaring winds and waters
block my path.
I fear!

Jesus: Fear not.
I'll light your way,
move mountains
from your path,
walk with you on waters
and teach you
how to laugh.

JESUS ONLY

Interviewer: As a person of faith,
what do you feel there is
in the Christian faith
that speaks most clearly
to the world today?

Charles Schulz: Always Jesus . . .
I think the minute we begin
to get away from Jesus himself,
we begin to cloud our theology.
I am a believer in the theology of
"Lord, let us see Jesus
and Jesus only."

This is why I refuse
to go out and speak to groups
as a so-called celebrity,
because I think anyone
who becomes religious
because somebody else is religious
is already on the wrong track.
A person should be converted
because he has seen
the figure of Jesus
and has been inspired by him.
And this is the only thing
that makes a person Christian.

Youth magazine

WE COULD NOT HEAR OR SEE

And
the Word of the Lord . . .
was a man
like unto
you and myself.

For we
could not hear
the song of the bodiless wind
nor see
our greater self
walking in the mist.

Jesus The Son of God
Kahlil Gibran
Published by Alfred A. Knopf, Inc.

DOOMED

If people do not get
their image of God
through Jesus,
it will not be a living image.
Any effort
to bring them back to God
without Jesus
is doomed to sterility.

SCARECROW GOD

Unfortunately, our idea of God
tends to be constantly downgraded.
As soon as one tries to hang on to it,
as soon as one fails to renew it,
to refresh it at its source
in Revelation,
it congeals, dries up, shrinks,
becomes a caricature,
a scarecrow, an idol.

All our natural ideas of God
are idols.
Men have been so wrong
about God
that he had to come
and tell them who he was:
"No one has ever known God . . .
It is the Son who has revealed him."

Our Prayer
Louis Evely
Herder and Herder

BETTER PICTURE

Without Jesus
we know little about
ourselves
our fellow man
or God.
We walk in
darkness and confusion.

PEANUTS & PAUL

Jesus
is the "word" of God
become man.

A word
welcomes and invites
communicates and reveals
tells us something.

Jesus is the word of God
because
he reveals something to me.
He does this
not only by what he says,
but by what he is.

Charles Schulz, the author of *Peanuts,* said:
"What Jesus means to me is this:
In him we are able to see God,
and to understand his feelings toward us."
St. Paul called Jesus
"the visible likeness of the invisible God."
Jesus himself said,
"Whoever has seen me, sees the Father."
Jesus is the Word of God,
because he reveals God to me.

But Jesus is the Word of God
in still another way.
Jesus reveals me to myself.
Jesus is the perfect picture
of what I should strive to be
He is the perfect image
of imperfect man.

Jesus is the Word of God
because he tells me
who God is,
who I am,
and what I can become —
if
I am open to his Spirit.

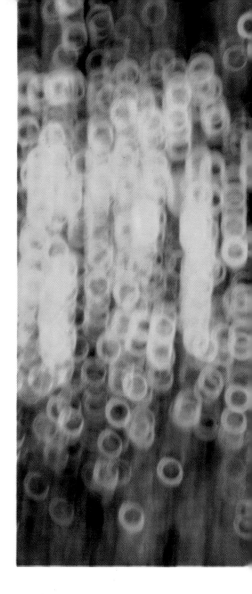

COSMIC WORD

When my thoughts take wing
and I think about the mystery
of the universe,
there dawns in my consciousness
a vague glimmering of what
the maker of the cosmos
must be like.

In a sense,
he left traces of
his "fingerprints" and "footprints"
on all that he touched —
planets, stars, and people.

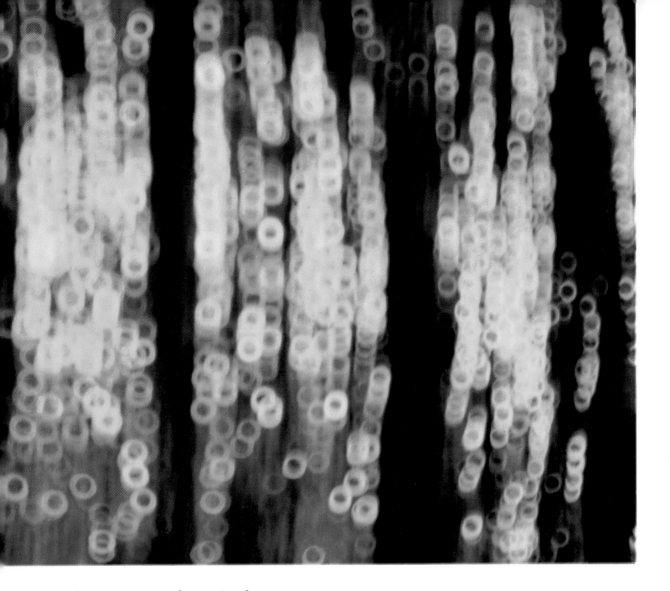

Just as a song sends out signals
of a songwriter's personality,
and just as house furnishings
reflect something
of an owner's personality,
so the cosmos mirrors
something of God.

In a sense,
the universe or cosmos
is God's "cosmic word"
to man.
It is the first "word" God spoke.
In the beginning, God said,
"'Let there be light.'
And there was light."

At that awesome moment
the "word" of God
was visibly translated
into the technicolor
universe of man.

Just as Jesus
is called a "word" of God,
because he reveals God to us,
so the universe may be called
a "word" of God,
because it, also, reveals to us
something of God.
It is God's "first word" to man.

INSPIRED WORD

The Scriptures
are God's "second word"
to man.
They have been aptly described
as the "word" of God
in the "words" of men.

The "word of God
in Scripture
is communicated to us

more through action
than through talk.

God frees his people
from slavery in Egypt.
He guides them
through the trackless desert.
He instructs them
through famines and wars.

In other words,
God did not merely *say*
he loved them.
He *showed* he loved them.
He did not merely *say*
sin is wrong.
He *showed*
it was wrong.

The word of God
in Scripture
is communicated to us
more through events
than through decrees.

The Bible is not a book.
It is a library of seventy-two books.
It is not a series of factual history books,
but a theologized history.
The men who God inspired
to write these books
did not intend to catalogue history;
they intended to interpret it.

They probed
beneath the surface
of historical events
and penetrated to the deeper meaning:
what God was telling men
through these events.

Just as the universe,
the "cosmic word,"
was God's first "word" to man,
so the Scriptures,
the "inspired word,"
were God's second "word" to man.

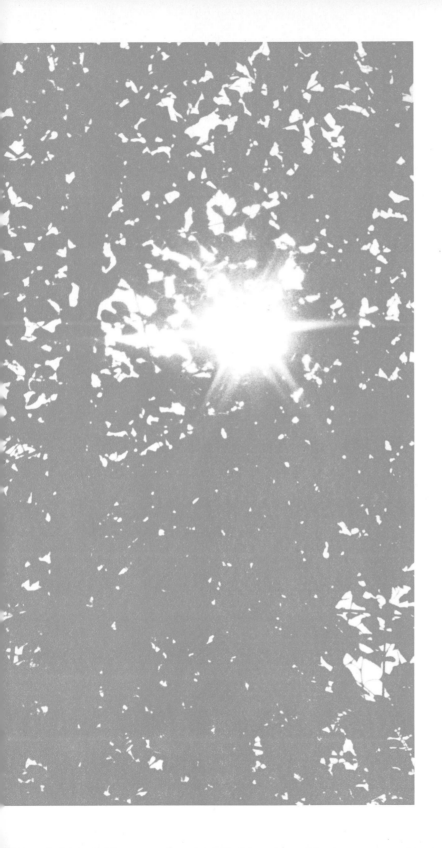

INCARNATE WORD

To understand
what St. John meant
when he called Jesus
the "word" of God,
we must keep in mind
God's "cosmic word"
and God's "inspired word."

Jesus is the third "word"
God speaks to man.
Jesus is
the "incarnate word,"
the "word" made flesh.

God has spoken to man
through three words.

the cosmic word
the incarnate word
the inspired word

Through these three words,
God reveals
himself to me and
me to myself and
my relation to other men,

Jesus is the fullness
of God's communication
to man.
He is the one word
that can
reach me.
challenge me,
change me.

REFERENCE POINT

In Jesus Christ
the reality of God
entered into
the reality of this world.

The . . . answer . . .
both to the question concerning
the reality of God
and to the question concerning
the reality of the world,
is designated solely and alone
by the name
Jesus Christ. . . .

Henceforward
one can speak
neither of God nor the world
without speaking
of Jesus Christ.
All concepts of reality
which do not take account of him
are abstractions.

Ethics
Dietrich Bonhoeffer

JUST ONE MAN
IN A SYSTEM

It was a rugged world . . .
Men were sold like lobsters
to die for others' amusement.
Rumors of insurrection
buzzed in cities and towns,
and at times
when walking along the road
one could see the results
of mass executions.

It was a sordid world —
of poverty contrasted with opulence,
of men literally used as fish food
while their masters
considered themselves aristocracy,
of women degraded,
of racial strife and hatreds.

. . . He came . . .
not as an emperor,
but as a low-born person,
to taste of poverty,
the sorrow,
the anguish,
to be just one man
in a system . . .

He . . . grew up
to become a revolutionary . . .
and in reaching out to people
with the *truth,*
He revolutionized . . . [the world]
by transforming individuals.

Reach Out
Tyndale House Publishers

CON
MAN

Jesus went out by the docks
and the man [the devil]
tried to con him.

He didn't eat for forty days —
and was starved.

After that the man came and said,
"OK, if you're the Son of God,
let's see you make
these red bricks
turn into bread."

But he didn't do it.
He just said, "Cool it, man,
you got to have more than bread
if you want to live big."

Then the man took him
to the steeple of St. Joe's.
The man says,
"Long way down, huh?
Lots of cars too!
Let's see ya jump.
Don't be chicken.
There's some cats with wings
to catch you."

But Jesus didn't do it.
He just said,
"Don't try to con God, man,
'cause you can't do it."

So the man takes him to
a big mountain
where he could see everything
and says,
"Feast your pincers on that.
I'll give you the whole thing
if you will worship me."

But Jesus wouldn't do it.
He just said, "I told you,
don't try to con God.

How many times
have I got to tell you
to cool it?
You are supposed
to worship God only."

So the man sees
he ain't getting switched on,
so he gets out of there and
Jesus gets some rest.

God is For Real Man
Carl Burke
Matthew 4:1-11 paraphrased
Published by Association Press

THE NEW ADAM

Through his encounter
with evil,
Jesus set the stage
for an understanding of

his identity and
his mission.

God said, "Adam,"
(which is to say "man")
"Be my son."
Adam said,
"No, Lord!"
Jesus' job is to
right Adam's wrong —
to restore man
to sonship
and love with God.

Like the "old" Adam,
Jesus is tempted to say, "No."
But where men before him failed;
Jesus succeeds.
St. Paul put it this way:

Through the old Adam
all men
were condemned to death.
Through Christ, the new Adam,
all men
are raised to life.

Romans 5:18

Besides being the new Adam,
Jesus is the new Israel.

Old Israel
wandered for forty years
in the desert
and fell into sins of sensuality,
presumption, and idolatry.

Jesus, the "new" Israel,
relives "old" Israel's history.

Like old Israel, he travels
forty days in the desert
(symbolic of the forty years).
Like old Israel,
he is tempted to sin.
But where they faltered
and failed,
Jesus succeeds.

After each temptation,
Jesus cites the Book of Deuteronomy,
where the three falls
of old Israel are recorded.

Jesus thus establishes
his identity
and his mission:
He is the new Adam,
head of a new family of men.
He is the new Israel
head of a new people of God.

Jesus, said,
"I am the way,
the truth,
and the life."

Jesus is:
the whole truth about God
the fullness of life from God,
the new way to God.

REAL IMPORTANT-LIKE

One day Jesus was hanging around down by the river.
There was some other guys who were friends
Of a square named John.

They takes a look at Jesus and says,
"There he is — God's man."

Jesus says, "So what's new with you?"
They tell him, "Not much.
But we hear you're a good Joe and we want
To join up with you.
Where is your pad?"

So Jesus says to them. "Come along and I'll show you."
And they did.
Jesus didn't tell them how stupid they were
Or call them retards —
He talked to them like they were real
important-like.

One of the cats was named Andrew.
He liked getting this kind of treatment
And goes and gets his brother.

His brother's handle is Simon and he is a fisherman.
Nobody thinks very much of fishermen
'cause they stink,
And that's for sure. . . .

When Jesus sees them coming he says,
"Your name is Simon, and your pop is named John."
Simon says, "Hey, how'd you know that —
who told you?"

Then Jesus says, "I'm gonna call you Peter."
This kinda shook Simon up, 'cause, even before
he could say a word,
Jesus knew all about him.

So he figures out that Jesus must be God's man
Just like Andrew says.

And he joins up with the gang, too.

The next day they all start for Jesus' crib.
On the way they meets a cat that they know
From their own turf —
His name is Philip.

Jesus says, "Come on, join up with us."
Well, Philip is out tracking anyway, so he joins up. . . .

Now Phil's got a friend — his name's Nathaniel.
Phil says, "Hey, Nat baby, we found the one
That 'The Book' told was coming.
He lives in Nazareth."

But Nat knows the Book pretty good and that God's man
Is supposed to come from Bethlehem.
So he says,
"You been sucked in pal,
Somebody is giving you a con job."

So Phil says,
"So OK, come take a look yourself."
And he did.

Jesus gives him the same treatment that Pete got.
He tells Nat all about himself.

Nat's no retard himself, so he figures out that
If Jesus knows this much and I didn't tell him anything
Either somebody's a stoolie
Or he is God's man.
And Nat joins up, too.

Then Jesus says to his new friends,
"You're gonna see some pretty big things from now on."

God is For Real, Man
Carl Burke
John 1:35-51 paraphrased
Published by Association Press

SOUL FRIENDS

If you wish to know
the heart and soul of another,
you must either
become his close friend,
or trust someone who is.

So it is with knowing Jesus.

The Gospels were written by men
who knew Jesus intimately.
Jesus revealed himself to them
in a deeply personal way.
He made them his witnesses.
"You are to bear witness,

because from the beginning
you are with me." John 15:27

The inner secrets
of Jesus' heart and soul
were entrusted
to his intimate friends.
We must either trust them
or have Jesus lost to us forever.

To accept Jesus
in isolation from his followers,
the early Christian Community,
would be unthinkable.
It would be to isolate oneself
from the source

NEW VISION AND POWER

There may be differences
in the way events in the Bible
are narrated.
There may also be variations
in the exact words attributed to Jesus.
But the important point is this:
The Bible converges
to give us
a unified portrait of Jesus.

In reading the New Testament,
we are struck by
its firmness of conviction.
The authors never write like philosophers,
groping for the final answer.
They never use the language
of doubt.
They transmit their message
as something that they experienced
with crystal clarity.

Here we must keep in mind
that nothing in Jewish tradition
prepared Jesus' followers
to accept what they later proclaimed.
Before becoming Christians,
they would have shrunk in horror
at the idea of divinizing
a fellow Jew.

of knowledge about Jesus.
It would be to do something
that Jesus never intended.

There can be no true
portrait of Jesus
except that
based on the witness
of his early followers.
Faith in Jesus
involves faith in the Christian community.

The Christian Community
is not the child of the
New Testament;
it is the mother.

The apostles were profoundly changed
by what Jesus communicated to them.
They were transformed
with new vision and power.

Two thousand years ago
the Gospel brought new life
to men in a world torn by strife
and disillusionment.
And today
each reader of the Gospel —
if he has the least spark
of imagination and idealism —
feels that it can do the same for him.

He is the still point of the turning world.

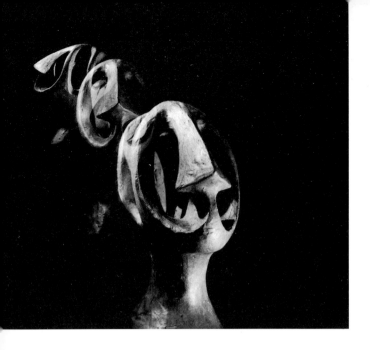

He frequently slept out under the stars.
Luke 9:58

These facts suggest
that Jesus was
physically fit and strong.

For these reasons,
many experts think we can say
that Jesus was attractive
and noble in appearance.
But the fact is
that we are not sure how he looked.

The important thing
is not how Jesus looked,
but who he was
and what he did,
and what he continues to do through us by the
power of his Spirit.

CONVERGING CLUES

What was Jesus like?
What kind of personality did he have?
How did he look?
People have often wondered
about these questions.
Though the Bible does not
describe how Jesus looked
or what kind of personality he had,
it does leave us some interesting clues.
For example,

Jesus held crowds spellbound for hours.
Mark 6:34-36

Children liked him.
Luke 18:15-16

Many people developed a deep affection for him.
John 11:1-6

These clues suggest
that Jesus had
an attractive appearance
and a warm personality.

Jesus lived a rugged life.
He walked miles in all kinds of weather.
John 4:1-6

He spent whole nights in prayer.
Luke 6:12

UNPREDICTABLE

[Jesus] constantly does
the most unexpected things,
revolutionizing
the accepted norms of conduct.

He praises pagans and prostitutes,
draws near to Samaritans and lepers.
He attacks
the most respected classes,
and insults his hosts at dinner.

In the midst of his intense labors
he finds time to welcome little children . . .
He rebukes the wind and the waves,
and falls silent before his accusers.

Men would never have fabricated
such a . . . religious leader,
and precisely for this reason
the Gospels have undying power
to convert humble hearts.

This spendthrift charity
is properly divine.
This is what God must really be,
and if he were to become man,
this is how he would behave.
Apologetics and the Biblical Christ
Avery Dulles

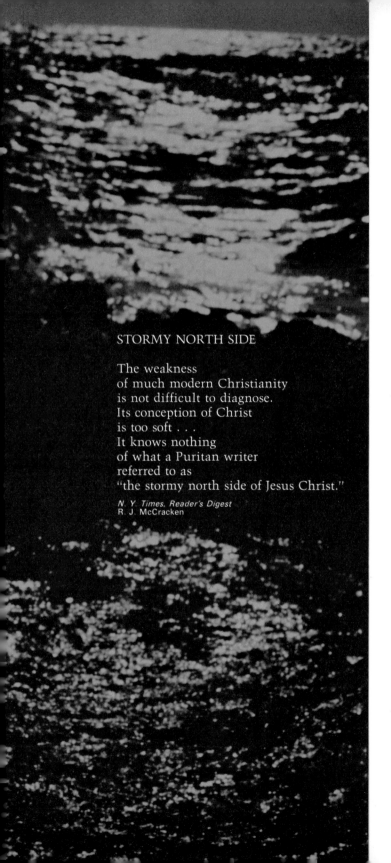

STORMY NORTH SIDE

The weakness
of much modern Christianity
is not difficult to diagnose.
Its conception of Christ
is too soft . . .
It knows nothing
of what a Puritan writer
referred to as
"the stormy north side of Jesus Christ."

N. Y. Times, Reader's Digest
R. J. McCracken

GOD, HE'S BEAUTIFUL

This Jesus.
God, he's beautiful.

I mean, he's really great.
He's not at all pretty
or "sick-beautiful"
like those pictures of him
that Christians hang on their walls.

He's not like that at all.
He's real.
He's got soul.

What he did is something else.
There's nothing like it.

You see,
when this Jesus came on the scene
God was like a stranger to people.
Oh, they thought they knew him,
but they didn't really.
Jesus knew him.
That's why he didn't fit in
with other people.
He was himself.
He didn't have to copy anyone.
He did what he had to do
and kept on doing it until
they couldn't take it any longer.
So they killed him.

He did his thing
because he was Jesus.
He wasn't trying to be someone else. . . .

He cut through all the phony ideas
of the priests and leaders
and told them the truth.
And he still does.
He really knows the truth about God,
and it's wild. . . .

This Jesus is beautiful.

Interrobang
Norman C. Habel
Fortress Press

3

THE FOCAL POINT OF A REVOLUTION

REAL COOL, MAN

Every place that Jesus went
he did some real groovy things
like fixing up busted bones,
or getting sick people better.
Every time he did it
some people said,
"Real cool, man!"
Some others figured
it was a fake
and he was a phony.
It sure scared the
hell out of some too.

God is Beautiful, Man
Carl Burke
Published by Association Press

The big question
is not how Jesus worked these miracles,
but why he worked them.
What point was he trying to make?
What was the deeper meaning
behind them?

To understand Jesus' miracles,
we must recall
that the Old Testament prophets
had predicted that a "new era"
would soon dawn
upon the world.

Describing how this era
would manifest itself,
Isaiah said,

Then will the eyes of the blind
be opened,
the ears of the deaf
be cleared;
then will the lame
leap like a stag;
then the tongue of the dumb
will sing.

Isaiah 35:5-6

This is precisely what Jesus did.
He opened the eyes of the blind,
made the deaf to hear,
and healed the cripple.

Thus when John the Baptist
sent a group of people
to ask Jesus
if he were the one promised
by the prophets,
Jesus said

Go bring word to John
about all you see and hear:
the blind recover sight,
the lame walk,
lepers are made clean,
the deaf hear,
dead men rise again,
the humble have the Good News
preached to them.

Luke 7:22

Jesus made it clear
that he was fulfilling
what the Old Testament prophets had foretold.
He was inaugurating the "new era."

Jesus also used other ways.
to teach this same truth.
He did this by demonstrating
his power over:

sin,
sickness,
and death.

These three evils
held mankind in slavery.
Jesus showed that he was freeing man
from this captivity by:

forgiving the sinner,
healing the sick,
restoring life.

Thus Jesus showed
power over man's weaknesses —
a clear indication that history
had turned a corner.
A "new era" was beginning.

SIGNS OF A REVOLUTION

Jesus' words', deeds and life style
were the trumpets of a new era.
They were the alarm clock of history,
jarring men from beds of apathy.
They were "signs" of a new day.
Jesus healed the blind.
But behind this miracle
was a deeper meaning.
It was a "sign" to all men to
open their eyes to
the bright light of a new day.

Jesus unplugged the ears
of the deaf. It too, was a "sign" to
all men to open their ears
to what he had to say.

Jesus forgave sinners.
Again, this was a "sign"
to all men to undergo a change of
heart and begin new lives.

Jesus' miracles were challenging and revolutionary.
Their purpose was to awaken the world — to set in
motion what he dubbed the "kingdom of God."
And what was this kingdom?
It was a new world order in which:

love would replace hate,
concern would replace unconcern,
light would replace darkness,
and life would replace death.
The revolutionary cry,
"Thy kingdom come,"
was to ring out and ring out.
Jesus told his people to:

shout it from housetops,
paint it in big letters
on weather-beaten walls,
sing it around night campfires,
chant it in the temple,
tattoo it on their hearts.

But more important,
Jesus told men to
do something about it.

This new era,
that shattered the silence of unconcern
and crumbled the walls of apathy,
was to be continued by men —
in a truly human way —
by living lives of love
and concern as Jesus did.
They were to show the world
what Jesus showed them:
that humanity was possible.

The hungry man,
the thirsty woman,
the naked child —
these would now find a brother,
where before they saw
only the shadow of a stranger
passing them like a ship in the night.

"I was hungry and you
shared your lunch with me;
I was thirsty and you
gave me half your coke;
I was cold and you
loaned me your sweater;
I was different and you
told the others not to make fun of me;
I was sick and you
explained my homework to me;
I was grounded and you
visited me.
As long as you
did it for one of these,
the least of my brethren,
you did it for me."

This was the revolution.
This was the sign.
This was the new miracle of history
that was to renew the face of the earth.

This revolution goes on.
Or does it?
Christians are called to be miracle workers —
transforming the world with their love and concern.
They are to be lightning bolts
and thunder claps.

But are they?
Why do so many of them
hide their light under a cardboard box?

Christians!
Where are you?
What's wrong with you?
Has the Spirit of Jesus
gone out of you,
as air leaves
a punctured balloon?

Or didn't you ever understand
what Christianity was all about?
Who will answer?
What is your excuse?
Is the revolution Jesus started
over or just beginning?

WE REFUSE TO BELIEVE

When Columbus discovered America,
some map makers refused
to put the new continent on their maps.
Until the late 1960's
the Flat Earth Society
refused to admit the earth was round.
When Ruth Cranston showed Chinese peasants
a photograph of the New York skyline,
they refused to believe what they saw.

This skepticism is a part of human nature.
When someone tries to teach us
about something that is new
and mind-blowing,
he can expect trouble.
He may be ridiculed
and looked upon as an oddball.

Jesus faced this problem
when he tried to tell people
who he was
and what he came to do.

Jesus' miracles had
a threefold "sign" value:
They were
signs of the beginning of a "new era",
signs of Jesus' concern for people, and
signs, challenging men
to take Jesus seriously.

THE POINT?

In his book, *Fire and Blackstone,*
John R. Fry, a black-ghetto pastor,
notes this about Jesus' response to
the blind beggar, Bartimaeus:

"Jesus did *not* ask him
how long he had been blind.
Jesus did *not* reach into his purse. . . .
He instead asked simply,
'What do you want me to do for you.' "

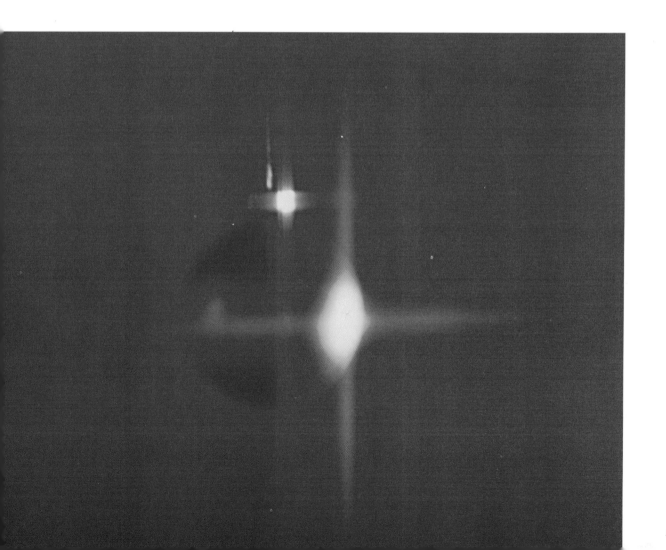

GOLD, NOT THORNS

In spite of his words and deeds,
many people refused
to believe in Jesus.
The reason?
They were unwilling
to put aside
their own pet notions
about what the "new era"
would be like,
and how
it would come about.

Most Israelites were looking
for a Messiah
who would make Israel
"number one"
among the nations.

They expected a Messiah
who would free Israel
in a political sense,
from things like military enemies.
They dreamed of a Messiah
who would catapult Israel
to wealth and power.

When Jesus told his people
that his kingdom
was one of the spirit,
most balked at the idea.
They wanted a material kingdom,
as well as a spiritual one.
They wanted a king
who would wear a crown of gold, not thorns.
They were disenchanted.
Jesus' teaching collided sharply

with their dreams of power.
So they closed their eyes
to his words and deeds
and stopped their ears
to his teaching.
This is why Jesus said:

So the prophecy of Isaiah
comes true in their case:

You will listen and listen,
but not understand;
You will look and look,
but not see.

Because this people's mind is dull;
They have stopped their ears,
And they have closed their eyes.

Matthew 13:14-15

THE DOOR

Who's going to open the door? . . .
God has opened the door,
and the door that is now open
is Jesus himself . . .
"I am the door,"
John 10:9

But what makes us angry
as we stand before this door,
is the very same thing
that made Charlie Brown angry:
there is no getting through this door
while still wrapped up
in our false securities.
All of us must first
be completely stripped
of all false gods
or false securities
before we can go through
that narrow door called "Jesus."
"We must throw off
every encumbrance,
every sin to which we cling".

The Parables of Peanuts
Robert Short

NO ACCESS

If the heart is devoted
to the mirage of the world,
to the creature instead of the Creator,
the disciple is lost. . . .

However urgently
Jesus may call us,
his call fails to find access
to our hearts.

Our hearts are closed,
for they have already been given over
to another.

The Cost of Discipleship
Dietrich Bonhoeffer

NOT READY

A brazen girl possessed of
seven devils was brought before
Jesus to be cured.

"I am going to cast out
those seven devils from you,"
he said.

"May I ask you a favor? . . ."

"What is it?"

"Cast out six."

Jesus Christs
A. J. Langguth

CLOSED!

Today most people
still turn off Jesus' words and deeds.
They have their own set ideas
about life and what it is for.
Their minds and hearts
have a "Do not Disturb"
sign hung across them.

One such person
said recently:

"There is only one thing
that would make me
even consider believing.
My own brother
would have to come back
from the dead
and tell me,
'There is life after death.
And it's just as Christ said it was.'"

Would this person begin to believe?
Or would he explain away
even this testimony?
Jesus himself, answered this question
by telling a parable.

There was once a rich man . . .
There was also a poor man,
named Lazarus . . .
The poor man died
and was carried by the angels
to Abraham's side,
at the feast in heaven;
the rich man died and was buried.
He was in great pain in Hades;
and he looked up and saw Abraham,
far away,
with Lazarus at his side.
So he called out,

Father Abraham!
Take pity on me and send Lazarus
to dip his finger in some water
and cool my tongue,
for I am in great pain in this fire!

But Abraham said:

Remember, my son, that in your lifetime
you were given all the good things,
while Lazarus got all the bad things;
but now he is enjoying it here,

while you are in pain.
Besides all that,
there is a deep pit lying between us,
so that those who want to come
over to us from here to you
cannot do it,
nor can anyone cross over
to us
from where you are.

The rich man said,
Well, father, I beg you,
send Lazarus to my father's house,
where I have five brothers;
let him go and warn them
so that they, at least,
will not come to this place of pain.

Abraham said,

Your brothers have Moses
and the prophets to warn them;
let your brothers listen
to what they say.

The rich man answered,

That is not enough, father Abraham!
But if someone were to rise from death
and go to them,
then they would turn from their sins.

But Abraham said,

If they will not listen to Moses
and the prophets,
they will not be convinced
even if someone were
to rise from death.

Luke 16:19-31

CHRIST POWER

Lord . . .
you who are divine energy
and living, irresistible might:
since of the two of us
it is you
who are infinitely the stronger,
it is you who must set me ablaze
and transmute me into fire
that we may be welded together
and made one.

Christ consumes with his glance
my entire being.
And with that same glance,
that same presence,
he enters those
who are around me
and whom I love.
Thanks to him therefore
I am united with them,
as in a divine *milieu* . . .
and I can act upon them
with all the resources of my being.

To read the gospel
with an open mind
is to see
beyond all possibility of doubt
that Jesus came to bring us . . .
not only a new life
superior to that we are conscious of,
but also . . . a new physical power
of acting upon our *temporal* world. . . .

If it is true
that the development of the world
can be influenced
by our faith in Christ,
then to let this power
lie dormant within us
would indeed be unpardonable.

Hymn of the Universe
Teilhard de Chardin

THE FOOL

If Jesus Christ were to come today,
people would not crucify him.
They would ask him to dinner,
and hear what he had to say,
and make fun of it.

Thomas Carlyle

WAITING

At your word I will let down the net.
Luke 5:5

The words and deeds of Jesus
are not actions of the past.
Jesus is waiting
for those who are still prepared
to take risks at his word
because they trust him.

4

THE TOUCH POINT
OF
ULTIMATE REALITY

I WONDER

"Nobody has ever talked
the way this man does."
John 7:46

Lately, I've wondered
what it must have been like
to look you straight in the eye, Lord,
and hear the sound of your voice.
Norman C. Habel

STILL IN THE WIND

The Greek and Roman orators
spoke to their listeners of life
as it seemed
to the mind.
The Nazarene spoke of a longing
that lodged
in the heart.

He knew the mountains
as eagles know them,
and the valleys as they are known
by the brooks and the streams.
And there was
a desert in his silence
and a garden in his speech.

To tell of the speech of Jesus
one must needs have his speech
or the echo thereof.
I have neither the speech
nor the echo.
I beg you to forgive me for
beginning a story
that I cannot end.
But the end is not yet
upon my lips.
It is still a love song
in the wind.

Jesus The Son of God
Kahlil Gibran
Published by Alfred A. Knopf, Inc.

REACHING OUT TO PEOPLE

Jesus faced an immense problem
when he tried to explain to the people
realities that were far beyond their experiences —
even imaginations.
He found himself in a position similar
to the teen-age girl in the novel,
The Heart Is a Lonely Hunter.

In one episode of the novel,
a teen-age girl is listening to a record.
As she listens,
she tries to explain to Mr. Singer,
a man who is deaf and dumb,
what music sounds like.
To do this,
she stands in front of him,
so that he can read her lips.
She also makes gestures with her hands
to get across her ideas.

After a while,
she gives up.
She realizes that
trying to describe sound to a deaf person
is like trying to describe color
to a blind man.

Jesus ran into this problem
when he tried to teach the people
about God
and the realm of the spirit.

It was like trying to describe
sound to a deaf man
or color to a blind man.
It was something
completely beyond their experience.
At best, Jesus could give
only a vague idea of
what it was actually like.

FISH STORY

One day a fish wanders off
from fish land.
He stumbles upon
submarines, divers,
and underwater cameras
invading the sea world.

Excited and alarmed,
the dumbfounded fish
returns to fish land
to spread the news
about these wierd invaders
from outer-water.

The poor fish is ridiculed
by the local experts, who say:
"But there can't be
intelligent life in outer-water!
Too much oxygen;
not enough water;
and the light would kill them.
What you saw were
probably refractions from
our own system."

This story was used by someone recently
to illustrate the possibility of UFO's.

Jesus used similar stories or
parables to help people bridge the gap
between the known and the unknown.
Jesus' parables stretched minds
and pushed back horizons.
People began to listen, to think,
and to question.

INSIGHTS

The parables of Jesus
are windows into
the mysterious world of God
and his relationship to man.

They are also mirrors
reflecting back to us
valuable data
about ourselves and our lives.

Four students meeting over a coke
discussed their opinion of the work of a
guidance counselor they shared.

Jan said that she didn't get much out
of the counselor. She didn't care
to share her problems with him.

Mike was more satisfied.
He told his counselor that,
because of their talk,
he had resolved to study harder.

He admitted that he had been
half-hearted in his approach to it.

Larry found the experience really helpful.
He talked to his counselor about several
problems, particularly his inability to read
with any speed or comprehension. He
arranged for special help.

Pat found the experience tremendous.
She mustered up courage to tell her counselor
about a family situation that had been bugging
her for over a year now. Her mother was an
alcoholic, and the physical and emotional
disturbance around the house made it impossible
for her to do any homework. It was the first
time she discussed it with anyone. She promised
to keep in touch with him about it.

Two months later, the four friends were
discussing this again. Compare their
conversation with the Parable of the Sower.

THE PARABLE

Hear, therefore, the parable
of the sower. When anyone
hears the word of the kingdom,
but does not understand it, the
wicked one comes and snatches
away what has been sown in his
heart. This is he who was sown
by the wayside.

And the one sown on rocky
ground, that is he who hears
the word and receives it immediately
with joy; yet he has not
root in himself, but continues
only for a time, and when trouble
and persecution come because
of the word, he at once falls away.

And the one sown among the
thorns, that is he who listens to
the word; but the care of this
world and the deceitfulness of
riches choke the word, and it
is made fruitless.

And the one sown upon good
ground, that is he who hears the
word and understands it; he
bears fruit and yields in one
case a hundredfold, in another
sixtyfold, and in another thirtyfold.

Matthew 13:18-23

REAL LIFE

Jan told the other three that
she had been given absolutely
no help. She didn't find the
counselor very relevant in the
first place. And in the second
place, who did he think he was,
nosing in everyone's business.

Mike said that he had kept his
resolution about study for three
weeks. He finally broke it, however,
when some of his buddies began to
"cut him down" about wasting his
life at his desk. The counselor is
all right but he doesn't understand kids.

Larry admitted that he had become
so involved in athletics
and social life that after a
month he had completely given up
on the reading improvement course.
"You can't be good at everything,"
he said. "I like the counselor
personally, but this school's teaching
methods are way out of date."

Pat was last to speak. She
told of how the counselor went
out of his way to give her and
her family some very sound advice.
Professional help was obtained for
her mother. She and her father were
advised how to help. Peace and joy
had returned to her home, thanks
to the counselor.

WRONG VALUES

I fear we are too much concerned
with material things
to remember that
our real strength
lies in spiritual values.

I doubt whether there is
in this troubled world today,
a single problem
that could not be solved
if approached in the spirit of
the Sermon on the Mount.

Harry Truman

IF

If you were to take . . .
all the authoritative articles
ever written . . .
on the subject of mental hygiene,
if you were to combine them,
and refine them
and cleave out the excess verbiage,
if you were to take
the whole of the meat
and none of the parsley,
and if you were
to have these unadulterated bits
of pure scientific knowledge
concisely expressed by the
most capable of living poets,
you would have an awkward
and incomplete summation
of the Sermon on the Mount.

The Case Book of a Psychiatrist
James T. Fisher

SERMON ON THE MOUNT

Jesus saw the crowds
and went up a hill,
where he sat down.
His disciples gathered around him,
and he began to teach them:

Happy are those
who know they are spiritually poor . . .
who mourn . . .
who are meek . . .
whose greatest desire is to do
what God requires . . .

Happy are those who
show mercy to others . . .
are the pure in heart . . .
work for peace . . .
suffer persecution . . .

You are like salt for all mankind. . . .
You are like light for the world . . .

You have heard
that men were told in the past,
"Do not murder;"
But now I tell you:
whoever is angry with his brother
will be brought before the judge . . .

So if you are about to offer your gift to God
at the altar
and you remember
that your brother has something against you,
leave your gift . . .
and go at once
to make peace with your brother;
then come back . . .

You have heard it was said,
"An eye for an eye,
and a tooth for a tooth."
But now I tell you:
do not take revenge on someone
who does you wrong. . . .

You have heard it said,
"Love your friends,
hate your enemies."

But now I tell you:
love your enemies, and pray for
those who mistreat you . . .

This is the way you should pray:
"Our Father . . .

Do not save riches here on earth,
where moths and rust destroy
. . . Instead,
save riches in heaven . . .
for your heart will always be
wherever your riches are.
No one can be a slave to
two masters . . .

Do not judge others
so that God will not judge you —
because God will apply to you
the same rules
you apply to others. . . .

Do for others what you want
them to do for you:
this is the meaning
of the Law of Moses
and the teaching of the prophets. . . .

. . . the crowds were amazed
at the way he taught.

Matthew 5:1-7:28

I HATE THE RULES

Why do I feel so sick inside,
so mad at myself?
And why do I want
to take out my feelings
on someone or something?
Why am I so confused
about what is right and what is wrong? . . .

God, If my parents ever knew
some of the things that go on in my head
I think they'd disown me!

They taught me the rules!
Don't steal! Don't swear! . . .
Don't answer back! Don't be rude!

And every time I break the rules
I sin, they say!
I am guilty!
I am wrong!
I am bad! . . .

But sometimes I'm not so sure
about the rules
or my parents
or the church . . .
or being born
or me!

I hate the rules
because, well, because they are just rules.
They are like squares on the floor,
like the circles of a target
at the rifle range,
like the lines running down the highway!

That's it!
They're like the lines on the highway,
double yellow danger lines,
and long white distance lines
and very hazy dotted lines
that vanish in the rain.

And so I've begun to wonder
about the rules
and the lines
and the rings.

What if those targets were really faces?
And what if those lines were really lives?
And what if those rules were really people?

Then sin would be breaking people
instead of breaking rules.
Sin would mean breaking up with God
instead of breaking his laws.
Sin would be personal
and cruel
and wrong. . . .

For Mature Adults Only
Norman C. Habel
Fortress Press

63

LAW CODES

The human person
has a tremendous potential for good.
Yet, he is also subject
to weakness and limitation.
All of us experience hate, envy, and greed.
Unharnessed, these drives
can destroy ourselves
and human society.
Man needs ethical motivation and guidance.
Looked upon in this way,
law codes serve a noble role
in human society.

THE FULFILLMENT

In Judaism, the Mosaic law code formed
the heart of Israel's life style.
The Law of Moses
was a remarkable achievement.
It underlined the fact that Israel's God —
unlike many ancient deities —
was a God of ethical concern.
"Be holy because Yahweh,
your God, is holy."
This ethical motivation made
the Law of Moses a unique document.

Jesus recast the Mosaic law,
making love its ethical motivation and thrust:
"Love others as I have loved you."
As God's self-revelation to man,
Jesus was the fulfillment
of what had been promised by the prophets.
"I have come not to destroy the law,
but to fulfill it."

Now if fulfillment means anything,
it means continuity, not reversal.
At the deepest level of human activity
what is morally wrong,
will never become morally praiseworthy,
or vice versa.

Murder, stealing, and dishonesty
can never be morally right.
Jesus does not abolish the old law,
he brings it to fulfillment.

FREEDOM

Jesus' concern was
human growth and freedom,
not legal conformity.
When Jesus taught morality,
he did so always in terms of love
and his Father's will.

Jesus loved the Father
and was totally open to his Father's will;
this was the whole thrust
of his teaching.
He taught men that
openness of the heart and spirit
is the way we become
what the Father invites us to be.

To clarify his Father's will,
Jesus frequently quoted Scripture.
But he never quoted
scriptural texts and laws
as if they settled all questions of
human conduct.
Jesus respected the law deeply,
yet his whole stance before it
differed from many of his contemporaries.
Legal structures were not meant
to bind or threaten man,
but to serve and liberate him.

OPENNESS TO THE SPIRIT

It was discovery of the "mind of Jesus"
that transformed St. Paul's attitude
toward the law.
After the year 50 A.D.,
Paul began to see the full meaning
of the cross of Jesus.
Up to this time, Paul had lived his life
under the law and was
deeply committed to its enforcement.
Now, he began to see that God was
accomplishing something entirely new
through his son, Jesus Christ.

For Paul, the law had become
a matter of pride, self-righteousness,
boasting, and false security.
Now, he saw that
accepting the mystery of the cross
— the "mind of Jesus" —
was just the opposite.
It was not making legally certain
where you stood with God.
Rather, it was forgetting about
heavenly "bookkeeping schemes"
and openning yourself joyfully
to an uncertain future — the Father's future,
guided by the Father's will.

Thus, St. Paul wrote:
"We . . . serve God in a new way,
the way of the Spirit,
in contrast to the old way,
the way of a written code."

Romans 7:6

For Paul, the ethic of Jesus
was not one of rigid conformity to the law,
but of flexible openness to the Spirit.
The sole purpose of law
was to facilitate this openness.
Jesus never intended to codify conduct
He was no moral minimalist,
He simply said,
"You can do more."
By this "more,"
he didn't mean more things.
He meant more trust — more love.
Having loved us first, the Father
can only invite our loving response.
"Love others as I have loved you."

Second, law serves as a spur to action,
when we are not as responsive to
love's invitation as we should be.
Just as Mother's Day or
Thanksgiving Day reminds us
that a love-response should be made,
so does law.

This then is the connection between
law and love: law is love's servant.

This puts a heavy burden upon
lawmakers and law enforcers.
They must always remember
that love does not do away with law,
but that law can do away with love.
Jesus demonstrated through his
life and message that
what could be written on hearts of flesh
could not be written on tablets of stone.

The foregoing selection are adapted in part from
"Does Love Do Away with Law" by Gerard Sloyan
in *So You're Having An Adolescent.*
Argus Communications

LOVE AND THE LAW

What then is the role of law
in the life of a Christian?
Law can never occupy more than a
secondary or supportive role.
It must always remain love's servant.
Law serves love in two ways.

First, it acts as a guide to action,
when we are not certain
what love invites us to do.
For the Christian does not always
find it easy to know
what love invites him to do.
He does not always hear clearly
what the Spirit is saying,
nor is he always open to the Spirit.

DOOR TO FAITH

Merely hearing about
the words and deeds of Jesus
does not produce faith.
They cannot force us to believe.
We are left free to accept
or to reject Christianity.
Recall the Pharisees
who witnessed Jesus' cure
of the blind man.
They refused to believe,
even though they had seen
the effect of the miracle
with their own eyes.
John 9:1-41

If we don't want to believe,
no one—
not even God—
can make us believe.

The words and deeds of Jesus can
make us stop and think.
They cannot
give us faith.
Faith will come to us
only in prayer.
The door to faith
is openness
to Christ in prayer.

WHY PRAY?

Prayer should not be thought of
as a means to an end.
True, it serves the noble purpose
of motivating us to live for God.
But, it is also an end in itself —
loving God.
Prayer is an expression of love —
complete and total in itself.

ALONE

But the news about Jesus spread . . .
and crowds of people came . . .
But he would go away
to a lonely place,
where he prayed.

Luke 5:15-16

At that time Jesus went
up a hill to pray, and spent
the whole night there
praying to God.

Luke 6:12-13

One time Jesus was praying
in a certain place. When he
finished, one of his disciples
said to him, "Lord teach us
to pray . . ."

Luke 11:1

THE PSALMS

Here are excerpts
from some psalms which Jesus
undoubtedly pondered
during his lifetime.

AN EVERYWHERE GOD

Psalm 139:7-11

How should I ever run away
from your spirit,
and where should I seek refuge—
you see me everywhere.
If I climb the heavens,
you are in the heavens,
if I go into the earth,
I find you there too.
And if I should fly
with the day-break
down to the uttermost shore of the sea,
there also your hand
will help me on,
there also your powerful hand
holds me tight.

A PERSONAL GOD

Psalm 139:1-16

My God, you fathom my heart
and you know me,
my God you know where I am,
where I go.
You see through my thoughts . . .
and you are familiar with
all that I do. . . .
I am known by you,
to the core, to my soul—
nothing in me was hidden
from your eyes . . .
and all of my life
was in your book
before one day of it
had been shaped.

A MYSTERIOUS GOD

Psalm 22:2-20

God, my God,
why have you abandoned me?
I cry out, and you stay far away.
"My God," I call all day—
you are silent.
I call through the night,
and you just let me call. . . .
you are so far away—
will you not help me,
are you not my strength?

A FORGIVING GOD

Psalm 32:3-6

As long as I was deaf
to the voice of my own conscience,
I was inwardly eaten up,
I took refuge in self-pity,
Your hand weighed heavily on me,
long days and nights. . . .

But then I could no longer
hide my evil from you.
I thought: I will go to him
and tell him what I have done—
and you forgave my sin.

A LOYAL GOD

Psalm 103:15-17

People—
their days are like grass,
they bloom like flowers
in the open field;
then the wind blows,
and they are gone
and no one can tell
where they once stood.
Only the love of God
will be lasting. . . .

A DESTINY GOD

Psalm 126

When from our exile
God takes us home again,
that will be dreamlike.
We shall be singing,
laughing for happiness . . .

Sow seed in sadness,
harvest in gladness.
A man goes his way
and sows seed with tears.
Back he comes, singing,
sheaves on his shoulder.

LEARNING TO PRAY

Our prayer . . . will succeed
only if we lose the very thought
of what we are doing
in the thought of him
for whom we are doing it. . . .
We succeed in prayer and in love
when we lose ourselves in both,
and are no longer aware
of how we are praying
or in what manner
we are loving.

On Prayer
Karl Rahner

One learns by doing.
Prayer is no exception.
The best (perhaps only) way
to learn to pray
is by praying.

WITH OR WITHOUT WORDS

We have all experienced
moments of prayer in our lives.
These experiences
may be compared
to what occasionally happens
to an amateur at sports.
A "Sunday" golfer
will sometimes get off a great shot.
An inexperienced basketball
player will sometimes sink a bucket
from thirty feet out.

So it is with all of us in prayer.
The fact that we did it once
means that we can do it again.
We have the capacity.

But like the amateur athlete
who must work to acquire
consistent skill,

we, too must work at prayer.
And although skill at sports
is not within the reach of all of us,
skill at prayer is.

Prayer normally takes three forms:
meditation,
contemplation,
and direct address.
Often these three forms
occur intertwined
in one and the same prayer —
like strands of wire coiled together
in one and the same cable.

In meditation
I ponder life
and the events of life
to seek God's presence and action
in my personal life
and in human history.

71

Meditation can lead to contemplation.
During such a prayer,
I am so struck with the idea of God
that I can hardly utter
a single word.
It is like enjoying a great piece of music
or gazing spellbound
at some fantastic view of nature.

Direct address
is the simplest form of prayer.
It is merely a response to God's presence
or a "calling out" to him
in his apparent absence.
Here is an example of direct address
from *Treat Me Cool, Lord,*
by Carl Burke.

There is no use
Giving a snow job to you, Lord.
You already know me like a book.

So when I'm all alone
Help me to see me like I am
Even if I don't like it.

Inside of me I want the right thing
Then when I'm with someone
I want them to think I'm the big man.

When I'm all alone tonight, God,
Help me to see
What you want me to be like.

STAY IN TOUCH

Some people feel
that prayer cannot be programmed.
It has to flow naturally,
like water from a cool spring.
If prayer does not flow spontaneously
from your heart,
you had better not pray at all.
Forced prayer is false prayer.

At first, this sounds convincing.
But when you take a closer look
at who man is
and how he operates,
you begin to see that
this is a simplistic position.

There is no question
that prayer sometimes comes unplanned
from within.
For example,
some unexpected good news
may send your spirits soaring.

Or some disaster strikes,
and you automatically turn to God.
Or you suddenly become aware
of God's hidden action
in some event.
When this happens
you stand still —
struck with awe and reverence.

The events of life
can lead you to God.
On the other hand,
just the opposite can happen.
Life can, at times,
stand like a massive wall
separating you from God.
Problems or failures
can so cloud your life
that you begin to see nothing
but gloom and darkness.
The saying that
"sorrow teaches people to pray"
is only half true.
Sorrow can so overwhelm
and embitter you
that you can't even stand
the thought of God.

Even success and temporary happiness
can obscure God
from your consciousness.
They can so take over your life
that you are no longer aware of God.
The realization of God's presence
can so completely vanish from your life
that you may go for months
without thinking of him.

If you hope to build your life
around spontaneous prayer only,
you may soon find yourself
not praying at all.
You run the risk of being like an athlete
who has tried to build his career
on spontaneous enthusiasm,
instead of training and practice.
Such a career would be fanciful.
It would be doomed to disaster
before it ever got off the ground.
The same is true of a person
who tried to build his spiritual life
on spontaneous prayer only.

PRAYER/ACTION

"There is a certain class of demons
that can only be chased away
by prayer" — the demons of
deafness to God,
dumbness in thanksgiving,
self-sufficiency, worry,
despair and solitude.

But there is another class
that can only be chased away
by action — the demons of
illusion,
sentimentality and infantilism,
narcissism and laziness.

So if we cultivate prayer exclusively,
we harbor the second lot,
and if we cultivate action exclusively,
we harbor the first lot.

Our Prayer
Louis Evely
Herder and Herder

LISTENING —
OF COURSE

Robert: How do you mean? voices?
Joan: I hear voices telling me what to do.
They come from God.
Robert: They come from your imagination.
Joan: Of course.
That is how the messages of God
come to us.
St. Joan
G. B. Shaw

Prayer is listening for God —
as well as speaking to him.
And if God is to speak to us,
it will be through our thoughts,
feelings, and imaginations.

Of course,
we cannot equate
all the movements of our interior
world with God.
But if God is to reach us,
it will be through the world of thought,
feeling, and imagination.

HOW DOES GOD TALK TO US?

I have heard so many
discouraged Christians say:
"The trouble is,
when I pray,
its just me talking.
God doesn't answer." . . .

God speaks to us through his Word,
but he also speaks to us
through the events of our life. . . .

If you look at your life —
the fact that you are reading this book . .
that you are still a Christian,
though perhaps you have
moved away from Christianity
at some stage and then back to it —
and all the varied circumstances
and sequences of life . . .

can't you see the pattern of a calling,
a faithfulness, a plan in it?

This is God talking
and he talks to us all the time,
though it is difficult
to make Christians understand this . . .

Even those who do not know God
sometimes recognize him suddenly
in the presence of a
truly religious person, happening,
or event.
They are suddenly forced to say:
"There is God." . . .
God talks to us at a level in ourselves
that we ourselves cannot reach . . .
an inner dimension that we did not
know we possessed
until he declared himself in it.

Our Prayer
Louis Evely
Herder and Herder

FOCUS

God is like space.
He permeates all reality.
And like space,
his presence is so pervasive
that we tend to overlook it
or take it for granted.

But God does more
than permeate reality.
He also uses created reality
as the vehicle of communication
with man.

If we are to find God
and communicate with him,
we must look for him in the world
and we must discover him
in the events of daily life.

Prayer might be compared
to what happens
when we tune a TV set.
Tuning merely brings into focus
signals that are already present.

Prayer is our point of contact, focus,
and communication with God.

ASKING FOR THINGS

I asked for health,
that I might do greater things,
I was given infirmity,
that I might do better things . . .
I asked for riches,
that I might be happy,
I was given poverty,
that I might be wise . . .
I asked for power,
that I might have the praise of men,
I was given weakness,
that I might feel the need of God . . .
I asked for all things,
that I might enjoy life.
I was given life,
that I might enjoy all things . . .

I got nothing that I asked for —
but everything I hoped for,
almost despite myself,
my unspoken prayers were answered.
I am among all men,
most richly blessed.
Author unknown

PRAYER IS NOT . . .

Prayer is not asking things of God,
but receiving what he
wants to give you;
it is not being heard by God,
but hearing God praying to you;
it is not asking God's forgiveness,
but opening yourself
to his forgiveness;
it is not offering yourself to God,
but welcoming God
offering himself to you.
Our Prayer
Louis Evely
Herder and Herder

TELL IT LIKE IT IS

In your prayers
do not use a lot of words,
as the pagans do,
who think that God
will hear them because
of their long prayers.
Do not be like them;
your Father already knows
what you need before you
ask him.
Matthew 6:7-8

LIKE IT IS

. . . I want you to listen
when I yell at the sky,
pound my pillow,
kick the ground,
throw stones at the stars,
slam doors,
or swear at the world.
Perhaps that's not giving
all glory to God,
as others do
with folded hands and frozen face,
but for me it means
I'm paying you
the highest respect there is.
It means I trust you with the truth —
all the truth.

"All Glory to God" in *Interrobang*
Norman C. Habel
Fortress Press

BOTH NEEDED

In his book, Honest to God,
John Robinson speaks of
two kinds of prayer times:
chronos, "time set by the clock," and
*kairos, "waiting for the moment
that drives us to our knees."*

In the past, writers have
emphasized the idea of
chronos-orientated prayer.
Robinson urges us to
investigate more fully the idea of
kairos-orientated prayer.

Author, Robert Raines,
points out that both forms of prayer
go hand-in-hand.
He refers to
kairos-orientated prayer as
"prayer-on-location" or
"street" prayer.
It is "prayer on the run" (*Are you
running with me,* Jesus?)
It is the gospel ideal of
"prayer without ceasing."
It is the Ignatian principle of
"finding God in all things."
It is openness and response to
God's presence in
the hectic events of daily life.

Raines refers to
chronos-orientated prayer as
"prayer-in-reflection" or
"stained-glass" prayer.
It usually takes place
in times and places of
solitude or worship.
It is the
"searching and deciding of Jesus"
on the mountaintop.
It is the
prayer of the community
in the temple.
It is the prayer
"before and after involvement."
It is the communal worship
of the Father.

Whereas
"prayer-on-location" is the
awareness/response
to the risen Jesus
present in life,
"prayer-in-reflection is the
awareness/response
to the risen Jesus
present in the Gospel.

ARE YOU RUNNING WITH ME, JESUS?

It's morning, Jesus.
It's morning,
and here's that light and sound
all over again.

I've got to move fast . . .
get into the bathroom, wash up,
grab a bite to eat,
and run some more.

I just don't feel like it, Lord.
What I really want to do
is to get back into bed,
pull up the covers, and sleep.
All I seem to want today
is the big sleep,
and here I've got to run
all over again.

Where am I running?
You know these things
I can't understand.
It's not that I need to
have you tell me.
What counts most
is just that somebody knows,
and it's you.
That helps a lot.

So, I'll follow along, okay?
But lead, Lord.
Now I've got to run.
Are you running with me, Jesus?

Are You Running with Me, Jesus?
by Malcom Boyd
Copyright © 1965 by Malcom Boyd
by permission of Holt, Rinehart and Winston, Inc.

5

THE PIVOTAL POINT OF HUMAN EXISTENCE

EATING TOGETHER

Food affects our lives
and our relationships with each other
more than we realize.
It draws people together.

THANKSGIVING MEAL

Food plays a unique role
in our relationship with God.
The focal point of Jewish history
is their "pass-over"
from slavery in Egypt
to freedom as God's chosen people.
The Jews
commemorate the event
with a "passover" meal
of thanksgiving.

The "passover" meal
not only celebrates a
memorial of a past event
but also
an anticipation of a future event —
the coming of the Messiah.

What the coming of the Messiah
meant to Jews
is expressed here by Jim Bishop:

[It] was a sweet national obsession.
It was ecstasy beyond happiness,
joy beyond comprehension;
it was balm to the weary farmer's bones
as he lay with his family
waiting for sleep;
it was the single last hope of the aged,
the thing a child
looked to a mountain of moving clouds
to see;

it was the hope of Judea in chains;
the Messiah was always the promise
of tomorrow morning.

The Messiah would effect
a new passover and a new covenant
Jesus was the Messiah —
the "awaited one" of Isreal.

On the night before he died,
Jesus met with his closest friends
to eat the old passover meal.
He used this occasion to inaugurate
the new passover and the new covenant.

"Jesus . . . took bread,
gave thanks to God,
broke it, and said,
'This is my body,
which is for you.
Do this in memory of me.'"

In the same way,
he took the cup . . . and said,
'This cup is God's new covenant,
sealed with my blood.
Whenever you drink it,
do it in memory of me.'
1 Corinthians 11:23-25

Within the framework of the old passover meal,
commemorating Israel's release
from *physical* slavery,
Jesus effected our release
from *spiritual* slavery.
He empowered us to "passover"
from a life of selfishness and unconcern
to a life of love and concern.

Thus the new passover and the new covenant
were inaugurated at a meal
which we now call the Eucharist.

JESUS OF NAZARETH
REQUESTS THE HONOR
OF YOUR PRESENCE
AT A DINNER
TO BE GIVEN IN HIS HONOR
TOMORROW MORNING.
ATTIRE IS INFORMAL.
RSVP

BROKEN/POURED

"Where did Jesus get that bread
and wine
that was used on the night
of the Lord's Supper?
Someone must have gone out
to the local baker,
to the wine shop
in Jerusalem,
and come home with a bottle of wine
and a loaf of bread . . .
They were dependent,
as we are today,
on the world
to provide us with the elements
within which we meet out Lord.

"Second, these elements are broken
and poured out.
It is the breaking of these things
and in the pouring out
that we see the dramatized way
in which Jesus is present
for us in the world . . .
We must focus on the action.
When Jesus took the bread
he broke it and said,
'This is my body
broken for you . . .'

"Third, the elements must be eaten,
taken into our systems.
Digested,
they become a part of our corpuscles
and molecules.
We do not 'observe' the bread
and wine;
we make them a part of our life.

Fourth, these elements are not
spiritual items,
but solid, substantial things
that you can get a grip on,
that you can see and eat."

God's Revolution and Man's Responsibilities
Harvey Cox
Published by Judson Press
Used by permission

YOU GO TO LEARN

You do not go to the Eucharist
to serve God;
you go to learn
how God breaks bread,
so that you can go
and do it in the same way,
because God is known
in the breaking of bread.

Our Prayer
Louis Evely
Herder and Herder

COMPLETELY ONE

Because the bread is one,
we, the many who all partake
of that one bread,
form one body.

1 Corinthians 10:17

By offering himself to us
under the form of food,
Jesus shows his desire
to be one with us.

By accepting Jesus' offering
of himself in the Eucharist,
we show our desire
to be one with him.

By sharing the Eucharist
with our fellow Christians,
we express and celebrate
our unity, in Christ,
with each other.

Jesus said:
"I pray that they may all be one. . . .
May they be one in us,
just as you are in me
and I am in you. . . .
completely one . . .

John 6:21-23

WOULD YOU LEAVE, ALSO?

"I am the bread of life,"
Jesus told them.
"He who comes to me
will never be hungry;
he who believes in me
will never be thirsty. . . .
I will never turn away anyone
who comes to me,
for I have come down
from heaven
to do the will of him
who sent me . . ."

"How can this man give us
his flesh to eat?" they asked.
Jesus said to them . . .
Whoever eats my flesh
and drinks my blood
has eternal life,

and I will raise him
to life on the last day.
For my flesh is real food,
my blood is real drink.
Whoever eats my flesh
and drinks my blood
lives in me
and I in him." . . .

Because of this, many . . .
turned back and would not go with him
any more.
So Jesus said to the
twelve disciples,
"And you —
would you like to leave also?"
Simon Peter answered him:
"Lord, to whom would we go?"
John 6:35-68

After the Supper,
Jesus and his apostles
climbed a hill
overlooking the city.

The hour of his passion was near.
Jesus prayed to be spared
the incredible inhumanity
that was to be poured upon him.

The spirit of his prayer, however,
is one of acceptance.
It is strikingly similar
to the "Our Father:"

"Father . . . not my will . . .
but your will be done."

WHERE YOU'LL FIND HIM

Newspaperman's advice to a youth
having faith problems:

"The darkness you are encountering
is in itself a rich experience.
If it be that you really want to meet Our Lord,
then it is by moonlight
that you must seek Him under an olive tree.
You will find Him flat on the ground,
and you will have to lie down on your face
with Him
if you are to catch His words.

The Way
Hugh Kay

ARREST

After Jesus finished praying,
a group of soldiers
came and
arrested him.

The following day
Jesus was sentenced
to death by crucifixion.

To curious onlookers,
Jesus' death was
just another Roman execution
of a Jew.
A modern newspaper correspondent
might have reported
the incident this way:

Jerusalem (AP)
Jesus of Nazareth
was executed today
outside the walls of the city.
Death came at about three o'clock.
A violent thunderstorm
scattered the curious crowd
of onlookers
and served as a fitting climax
to the brief but stormy career
of this self-styled preacher
from the hill country.
Burial took place
shortly after the storm subsided.
A police guard
has been temporarily assigned
to the grave site,
as a precautionary measure.
The Nazarene is survived
only by his mother.

DEEPER MEANING

But there was more
to Jesus' death
than an AP release
might have carried.
Below the surface
lay a deeper meaning.

Just before Jesus died,
a sponge soaked in wine,
was lifted up to him
on a stalk of hyssop.

A hyssop stalk
held a special significance
for Jews.
It was the instrument used
to smear lamb's blood
on Israelite doorposts
at the first Passover.
Symbolically, it now connected
the Old Passover
with the "New" Passover.

At the hour of Jesus' death
". . . the curtain of the temple sanctuary
was torn in two
from top to bottom."

For centuries the Jerusalem temple
symbolized God's presence
among his people.

The tearing of the curtain
symbolizes God's departure
from the temple.
The Old Testament temple and sacrifice
are now ended.

Jesus gave us a new temple
and a new sacrifice.

The new temple
will be his mystical body —
the Christian community
for all mankind.
The new sacrifice
will be his own sacrifice,
as Jesus instructed us
to commemorate it
at the Last Supper.

LOVE — BEYOND SUFFERING

Mark ends his gospel account
of the crucifixion.
by quoting an "army officer,
who was standing there
in front of the cross."
The officer cries out,
"This man was really the Son of God."
Mark 15:39

The suffering of the cross
is not meant for itself
but for something else.
Christ does not suffer
because suffering is in itself a value
but because love without restraint
requires suffering.

It is not a love for suffering
which Christ reveals
but a love which prevails in suffering
It is not the physical death of Jesus
which is redemptive
but the love of Jesus for us
even unto death.

The death of Jesus reveals to us
how absolute God's love is.
God's love is conditionless,
expressing itself even to the point
of ultimate donation in death.
We are saved not by
the physical death of Jesus
but by the absoluteness of a love
which did not count death
too high a price.

The love of Jesus
is redemptive
in its absoluteness
and victoriously communicative
in the Resurrection.

The crucified Jesus
is a sign that Christian love
lives in a threatened situation.
He shows us
that if we accept all the circumstances
of love,
love may suffer
but it overcomes.

The man of faith
has found a hope
stronger than history
and a love
mightier than death.

Who is Christ?
Anthony Padovano

BEYOND DEATH — LIFE

I gazed into the visions
of the night.
And I saw,
coming on the clouds of heaven,
one like a son of man.
He came to the one of great age
and was led into his presence.

On Him was conferred
sovereignty! Glory and Kingship . . .
His sovereignty
is an eternal sovereignty
which shall never pass away,
nor will his empire
ever be destroyed.

Daniel 7:13-14

if the gospel we preach is hidden,
it is hidden only to those who . . .
do not believe because
their minds have been kept in the dark
by the evil god of this world.
He keeps them from seeing
the light shining on them,
the light that comes from the Good News
about the glory of Christ,
who is the exact likeness of God.

2 Corinthians 4:3-4

No longer, then, do we judge anyone
by human standards.
Even if at one time we judged Christ
according to human standards,
we no longer do so.
When anyone is joined to Christ
he is a new being:
the old is gone,
the new has come.

2 Corinthians 5:16-17

In the past, we have tended
to think of Jesus' death and resurrection
as two separate events.
This is something the biblical writers
never intended.
They saw Jesus' death/resurrection
as an inseparable whole —
the "paschal mystery."

The paschal mystery is
humanity's victory.
Jesus' death/resurrection
frees and empowers us
to live as a new creation in Christ.
It makes our humanity possible.

HUMANITY IS POSSIBLE

I am the vine,
you are the branches.
Whoever remains in me,
and I in him,
will bear much fruit;
for you can do nothing
without me.

John 12:24

To be truly human
is to be conscious
of human weakness,
but confident
that it can be overcome.

Romano Guardini

Our chief want in life
is somebody
who shall make us
do what we can.

Ralph Waldo Emerson

As I have loved you
so you
must love one another.

John 13:34

People are lonely
because they build walls
instead of bridges.

J. F. Newton

the man who
wants to save his own life
will lose it;
but the man who loses his life
for my sake will find it.

Matthew 16:25

There's something
about a man
who has fought for it —
I don't know what it is —
a look in his eye —
the feel of his hand.
He needn't have been successful —
though he
probably would have been. . . .
If you had kept on —
if you had loved it enough
to keep on —
fighting and struggling
and sticking it out —
why that fight
would show in your face today —
in your eyes and your jaw . . .

You're all smooth.
I like 'em bumpy.

So Big
Edna Ferber

I pray that they
may all be one. . . .
May they be one in us,
just as you are in me
and I am in you. . . .
completely one . . .

John 6:21-23

I sought my God,
but my God I could not see.
I sought my soul,
but my soul eluded me.
I sought my brother,
and found all three.

Author unknown

If you have love
for one another,
then all will know
that you are my disciples.

John 13:35

Example
is the school of mankind
and they will learn at no other.

Edmund Burke

a grain of wheat
is no more than a single grain
unless it is dropped
into the ground and dies.
If it does die,
then it produces many grains.

John 12:24

Fear not that your life
shall come to an end,
but rather that it shall never
have a beginning.

John Henry Newman

This is my commandment:
love one another
just as I love you.

John 15:12

In the book, *The Sands of Dunkirk,*
Surgeon-Lieutenant Richard
Prembrey wept as he watched
a dying soldier
strip off his own blanket,
and place it across the
shivering body
of a pneumonia-strickened trooper
in the next bunk.

No servant can be the slave
of two masters . . .
Luke 16:13

Man is too noble
to serve anyone but God.
Newsweek
Cardinal Wyszynski

I have come in order that
they might have life,
life in all its fullness.
John 9:9-1

The enemy of the best
is not the worse,
but the good enough.
L. P. Jacks

If you love only the people
who love you,
why should you
expect a blessing?
Luke 6:32

Sometime ago
a magazine carried a photograph
of a man prostrate on a subway stair.
For thirty minutes
people passed by without
giving him a hand.

Love your enemies,
do good to those
who hate you . . .
and pray for those who
mistreat you.
Luke 6:27-28

Could we read
the secret history of our enemies,
we should find
in each man's life,
sorrow and suffering enough
to disarm all hostility.

William Longfellow

FREEDOM "NOW"

Man
cannot free himself;
he must be set free,
and this can happen only because
God has given himself
for us
in Jesus Christ.

This saving act of God, however,
is not in the distant past,
for the liberating event takes place
when a man
responds to the word of the cross
by deciding
to understand himself
as crucified and dead
to his own past
and open solely
to the future offered to him
in that word.
The Secular Meaning of the Gospel
Paul M. van Buren

TAKE CHARGE

God says:

Dominate nature
and make it subject to you . . .

You are not a slave
whose duty is to thank me
and respect my work;
you are my son,
you take charge,
you work with me,
and you take the responsibility
and the initiative.
Our Prayer
Louis Evely
Herder and Herder

God's plan,
which he will complete
when the time is right,
is to bring all creation together,
everthing
in heaven and on earth,
with Christ as head.
Ephesians 1:10

FREE TO FREE

Christ is just as much
the revelation of man
as the revelation of God.
Being so truly God
made him the only true man
who has ever lived . . .
This why . . .
we take heart and say:

"Our Father . . .
"You have
shown and taught us your love . .
that we can pass it on . . .

"You have shared your bread
with us so well
that you have made us capable
of sharing ours as well;

"You have forgiven us so well
that you have taught us . . .

"And with you, in you
and through you,
we will free the world from evil."

Our Prayer
Louis Evely
Herder and Herder

TERMINAL POINT

In Jesus Christ,
true God and true man . . .
rests our hope for real humanity.
Not by ourselves,
but insofar as we are members
of the Body of Christ . . .

In order to . . . be man . . .
we must believe in Jesus Christ.
There is no humanism
without the Gospel.

The Faith of the Church
Karl Barth

Christ
is the terminal point
at which, supernaturally
but also physically
the consummation of humanity
is destined to be achieved.

Hymn of the Universe
Teilhard de Chardin

YOUR BROTHER IS WAITING

. . . Christianity is the good news
that God loves the unworthy,
that he does not need us to be worthy
in order to love us.

And the consequence is vital:
you will behave like your God.

If you wait for your brothers
to become worthy of being loved,
you will wait for the rest of your life.
Because they are waiting
for you to love them
so they can be worthy of your love.
They need to be loved
if they are to become better.

Our Prayer
Louis Evely
Herder and Herder

IMPOSSIBLE DREAM?

Each time
a man stands up for an ideal,
or acts to improve the lot of others,
or strikes out against injustice,
he sends forth a tiny ripple of hope.

And crossing each other
from a million different centers
of energy and daring,
those ripples build a current
that can sweep down
the mightiest walls
of oppression and resistance. . . .

Moral courage
is a rarer commodity
than bravery in battle
or great intelligence.
Yet
it is the one essential vital quality
for those
who seek to change a world
that yields most painfully to change.

Robert Kennedy

You see things
as they are; and you ask "Why?"
But I dream things
that never were:
and I ask "Why not?."

G. B. Shaw

To dream
the impossible dream,
to fight
the unbeatable foe . . .

This is my quest
to follow that star,
no matter how hopeless,
no matter how far . . .

Mitch Leigh and Joe Darion

FREE AT LAST

Universe
and every universe beyond,
spin and blaze,
whirl and dance,
leap and laugh
as never before.
It's happened.
It's new.
It's here.
The liberation.
The victory.
The new creation.
Christ has smashed death.
He has liberated the world.
He has freed the universe.
You and I and everything
are free again,
new again,
alive again.

Let's have a festival
and follow him across the skies,
through the flames of heaven
and back down every alley of our town.
There, let's have him come
to liberate our city,
clean up the mess
and start all over again.
You conquered.
Keep on fighting through us.
You arose.
Keep rising in us.
You celebrated.
Keep on celebrating with us.
You happen.
You are new.
You are here.

"Easter" in
Interrobang
Norman C. Habel
Fortress Press

AND YOU'LL WANT
TO TRAVEL WITH HIM

And you want to travel with him,
And you want to travel blind
And you think maybe
you'll trust him
For he's touched your perfect
body with his mind.

Leonard Cohen

To those who wish to travel
with him, Jesus says,
"Give up your Linus-blankets:"

your pride,
your selfishness,
your comfort.
change your heart.

"REPENT"
Luke 3:3

"BE BORN AGAIN"
John 3:3

"BECOME AS CHILDREN"
Luke 18:17

"FOLLOW ME"
Mark 10:31

"PICK UP YOUR CROSS"
Mark 8:34

"DIE TO YOURSELF"
Mark 8:35

TOUCHIN' IS BELIEVIN'

After Jesus busted outa the grave
He met two of his gang on a road.

Man! were they ever spooked and surprised.

They ran like crazy to the place where the other
guys were.
And started to tell who they seen.

Before they could say much, bingo!
Jesus was there,
Came right through the door,
And they couldn't figure that out either.

He said, "Peace!"

Good thing to say 'cause they was plenty scared
Knees shakin' and teeth jumpin'.
They thought for sure, this is a ghost.
And who wouldn't?

So Jesus says,
"What buggin' you?
I ain't no ghost."

"See, I got hands
And feet just like you guys.

Go ahead, touch me and see.
You know seein' is believin'."

Well, they couldn't fight that; so they believed,
But, man, were they still surprised. . . .
Who wouldn't be to see someone
Who busted out of a grave?

One of the Jesus gang was not there —
He musta been real beat
And was out hanging around the corner
Or maybe out tracking another gang.

He thought that the Jesus gang was all washed
up anyway.

He didn't have no place to go
An' nothin' to do
So he went up where some of the Jesus
gang were. . . .

"Betcha can't guess who was here."
Thomas says, "So who cares?"

The rest of them says, "Jesus was here."

Thomas says,
"Whats a matter with you guys,
You trying to be funny or something?"

Well, the rest of the guys finally get it through
His thick head that they did see Jesus.

So Thomas says, "All right, all right, so you
saw him,
But I ain't believing till I
Touch him.
Is that so bad?"

About a week later the Jesus gang
Was in the same room again. . . .
Thomas ain't takin' no chances this time,
So he goes to the meetin'.

Sure enough Jesus came again . . .
Thomas' eyes almost bugged out when he saw
Jesus.

He just looked and looked
And he says to himself,
How about that?
They did level with me.

Jesus knows that old Thomas is having trouble
Believing about him still being alive.

He didn't yell at him
Or bawl him out,
Or tell him he was no good,
Or swear at him.

He just walks over and says,
"Evening, Thomas,
I just want to help you.
Don't be scared.

"Just touch me and you'll see I'm for real."
So Thomas did touch him
First, his hands
Then his side,
Right where he got stabbed.

That did it,
Thomas knew the rest of them was right
And he was just as happy as the rest.

Thomas says, "You are for real!
You're the Lord!"

Jesus says,
"You believe 'cause you see me.
People who believe without seeing me
May have it hard too,
But that makes it better for them."

God is For Real, Man
Carl Burke
Luke 24:36 and John 20:19-30 paraphrased
Published by Association Press

HALLUCINATIONS

Historians who reject
the doctrine of Christ's resurrection
most commonly maintain
that the apostles experienced
hallucinations of some sort. . . .
Prof. William Albright, . . .
an eminent historian,
has some . . . reflections on the point
in his *From Stone Age to Christianity* . . .

What we have in [the Gospels] is . . .
a reflection of reports of eye-witnesses
who were overwhelmed
by the profound experiences
and the extreme tension
of mind and body through which
they had passed.

Men who see
the boundary between
conventional experience
and the
transcendental world
dissolving before their very eyes
are not going to distinguish clearly
between things seen
in the plane of nature
and things seen
in the world of spirit.

To speak of the latter
as "hallucinations"
is quite misleading . . .
Here the historian has no right
to deny what he cannot disprove.

Apologetics and the Biblical Christ
Avery Dulles

TURNABOUT

When Jesus lived,
the Jews were under the political heel
of Rome.
Jesus came into history
at the very hour
when Rome was taking a census
of the Jews.

In almost every region
of the Roman Empire
it was possible to deify a man.
But there was one place
where this was utterly impossible.
That was in Israel.

The Jews were monotheists.
They believed in only one God.
This explains why there was
only one temple in Israel —
the Jerusalem temple.
This also explains why
the Jews never allowed
images of God
to be made.
To link God with any image
or any man
was absolutely unthinkable.

The Jews honored the Roman emperor,
but they would have
let themselves be destroyed
rather than profess,
that he might be god.
So, too, the Jews honored Moses,
but they would have died
rather than think
that he might be God.

How is it possible to explain
the incredible turnabout
in Jewish religious tradition
that took place among Jesus' followers
after Jesus' death.
Only if Jesus were God,
could this extraordinary
phenomenon have taken place —
in of all places, Israel.

YOU COULDN'T STOP THEM

Considerable variation occurs
among the Gospel accounts
[concerning the resurrection, but] . . .
one central fact continues to emerge.
All the persons most intimately associated
with the early Christian movement
were convinced beyond doubt
that Jesus rose from the dead.
The exact nature of the experiences themselves
can never be known.
Were they subjective or objective?

A historical approach
to the subject
cannot answer these questions,
but the shadow of uncertainty
in this area
is more than cleared
by the light of certainty
in the basic conviction
which the appearances proclaimed.
From that time on
the men of Palestine
who had been Christ's followers
never wavered from the faith.
They were totally convinced
that Jesus Christ was the Messiah
and that he had indeed cheated death . . .

Off they went with burning urgency
to tell the news to all the world.
The Messiah had come.
Truly the Kingdom of God
was at hand.

Their lives were led for that end,
and for that end alone.
No amount of persecution
could stop them . . .

Many were to find crosses of their own
on which to hang.
Some were torn apart
by wild beasts in the arena.
Others were burned alive,
but the basic conviction
remained unchanged.

An Analytical Approach to the New Testament
F. B. Rhein

Had these unlearned men
cunningly devised
a fictional message
(a scheme for which they had
no discoverable motive),
it would be reasonable to assume
that sooner or later
one or more of the eleven
(not to mention other followers)
would have confessed the subterfuge
under the pressure
of numerous threats of death.

But none did.
Their witness never wavered.
Rather, they experienced an
amazing power that even
enabled them to work miracles!

The lives and message
of these men changed the course
of human history.
No reasonable explanation
has ever been given
to account for their transformed lives
except their own:
they had seen Jesus
alive . . .

Hope in *the Midst of Horror*
Robert L. Cleath
Copyright 1970 by *Christianity Today;*
used by permission

ALIVE!

Christ's followers
were utterly distraught
by [his] . . . execution . . .
and they feared
for their own safety,
because of the violence
of Christ's enemies.

Yet in a matter of days
these discouraged and
frightened men
were amazingly transformed.
They openly and fearlessly
proclaimed Christ alive
from the dead. . . .
So strong was their belief
that they submitted
to persecution and death
rather than deny their Lord.

LET LOOSE

In John Masefield's
The Trial of Jesus,
the following conversation
takes place
between the centurian
who stood beneath the cross
and Pilate's wife:

"Do you think he is dead?"

"No, lady, I don't."

"Then where is he?"

"Let loose in the world, lady,
where neither Roman
nor Jew
can stop his truth."

DID YOU EVER DOODLE?

Lord,
did you ever do something silly,
just for the fun of it?

For example,
did you ever sit
and doodle in the air
floating somewhere
before you had this heavy world
upon your hands?

Did you ever let yourself go
and take a wild ride
across the galaxies
or tie a rainbow up in knots
without a thought
of just what someone else
might think of you?

Are the platypus and the kangaroo
a couple of favorite jokes
you kept for laughs? . . .

Come on, God! . . .
Let's loosen up the world a bit
and use the fireman's hose
to knock the hats
off all those cats
who stiffen up their backs
and think they own this town.

Let's stop the traffic for a day
and have a ticker-tape parade
for all the orphans we have made.
Let's turn the land into a fair
and throw confetti in the air
to celebrate that you have come
to join us here.

Come on, God, let's go.

If Jesus Christ means anything
it means he's one of us
And if his resurrection
isn't just a dream for dying men
then he's the one
who has to come
and bring this globe to life again.

Interrobang
Norman C. Habel
Fortress Press

END-POINT

Thus all the lines converge,
complete one another,
interlock.
All things are now but one.

Lord . . .
when it was given me to see
where the dazzling trail
of particular beauties
and partial harmonies was leading,
I recognized that it was all
coming to center on
a single point,
a single person: yourself.

Christ is the end-point . . .
of the evolution,
even the *natural* evolution,
of all beings;
and therefore
evolution is holy.

Hymn of the Universe
Teilhard de Chardin

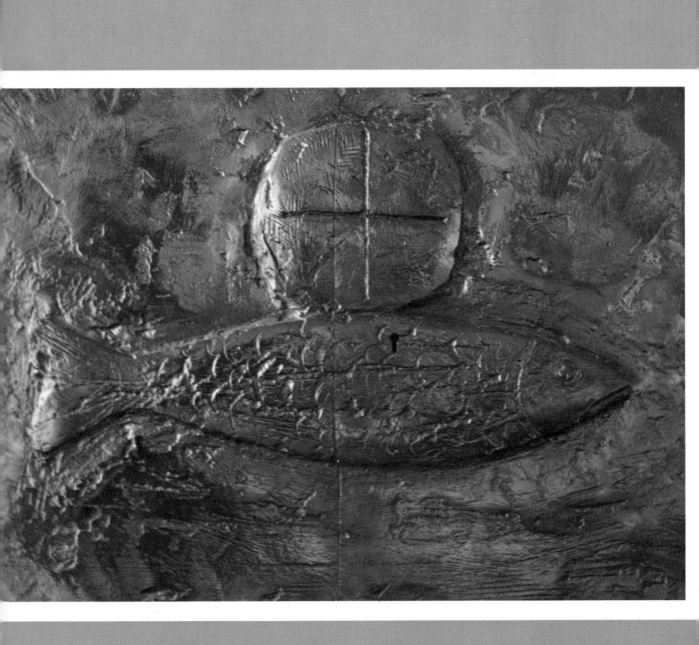

6

THE DECISION POINT
IN
EVERY LIFE

THE WAY

When we have
traveled all ways,
we shall come
to the
End of all ways,
who says,
"I am the way."
St. Ambrose

I AM A CROWD

Within my earthly temple,
there's a crowd;
There's one of us that's humble,
and one that's proud;
There's one that's
broken-hearted for his sins
And one who
unrepentant sits and grins.

There's one who
loves his neighbor as himself;
And one who
cares for naught but fame and self.
From much corroding care
I should be free,
If once I could decide
which one is me.

Author unknown

WHY?

Judas:
Everytime I look at you
I don't understand
why you let the things you did
get so out of hand.
You'd have managed better
if you'd had it planned . . .
Don't you get me wrong—
I only want to know.

Jesus Christ—Superstar
A Rock Opera by
Andrew Lloyd Webber and Tim Rice

ONE WORD

Words! Words! Words!
Like harmless bullets
fired at my brain.
God words! Big words! . . .
Long words! Lost words.

I've learned the words . . .
and memorized the words
until I'm full of words.
They're plastered across my brain
like stickers on a billboard.

But they're only words.
I don't know what they mean
or where they belong. . . .

Status

Security

Fame

Happiness

Power

Money

Service

Truth

Acceptance

Fear

Love

Commitment

Personality

Fortune

Meaning

Words are everywhere.
People spit them out
all the time
and most of the time
they are wasted.
There are millions of words
spinning through the air,
millions of sound waves
crashing against each other
and saying nothing!

Lord
is there one word,
one word strong enough
to get through all the other words
and reach me.
Is there a word that can
get under my skin
and reach me
and change me?

Is there one word
with a face and hands
and power and life,
one word I can meet head-on?

Is there one word
that will not fall through
the cracks into my subconscious
and die?
Is there one word like that?
One solid word?
Is there?

For Mature Adults Only
Norman C. Habel
Fortress Press

THE WORD

Before the world was created,
the Word already existed;

he was with God,
and he was the same as God.

From the very beginning,
the Word was with God. . . .
The Word had life in himself,
and his life
brought light to men. . . .

The Word, then,
was in the world. . . .
yet the world did not know him . . .
The Word became
a human being
and lived among us . . .
Jesus Christ.

John 1:1-7

TEST OF GREATNESS

To millions of persons,
Jesus is more than a man.
But a historian
must disregard this fact.
He must adhere to the evidence
that would pass unchallenged
if his book were to be read
in every nation under the sun. . . .

Yet, more than 1900 years later,
a historian like myself,
who doesn't even call himself
a Christian,
finds the picture centering
irresistibly around the life
and character
of this most significant man.

We still catch something
of the magnetism that induced men
who had only seen him once
to leave their business
and follow him.
He filled them
with love and courage.
He spoke with
a knowledge and authority
that baffled the wise.

But other teachers
have done all this.
These talents alone
would not have given him
the permanent place of power
which he now occupies;
that place is his
by virtue of the new and . . .
profound ideas
which he released.

It is one of the most revolutionary
changes of outlook
that has ever stirred
and changed human thought.
No age has even yet
understood fully
the tremendous challenge
it carries . . .
But the world began to be
a different world
from the day that doctrine was preached,
and every step
toward wider understanding . . .
is a step in the direction
of that universal brotherhood
Christ proclaimed.

The historian's test of
an individual's greatness is
"What did he leave to grow?"
Did he start men to thinking
along fresh lines with a vigor
that persisted after him?

By this test
Jesus stands first.

The Three Greatest Men in History
H. G. Wells, *Reader's Digest*

ONE SOLITARY LIFE

Here is a man
who was born of Jewish parents
the child of a peasant woman. . . .
He never wrote a book.
He never held an office.
He never owned a home.
He never had a family.
He never went to college.
He never put foot
inside a big city.
He never travelled two hundred
miles from the place
where he was born.

He never did one of the things
that usually accompany greatness.
He had no credentials
but himself. . . .

While still a young man,
the tide of popular opinion
turned against him.
His friends ran away.
One of them denied him. . . .
He was nailed to a cross
between two thieves.
His executioners gambled for
the only piece of property
he had on earth . . . his coat.
When he was dead
he was taken down
and laid in a borrowed grave
through the pity of a friend.

Nineteen wide centuries
have come and gone
and he is the centerpiece
of the human race and the
leader of the column of progress.
I am far within the mark
when I say that all the armies
that ever marched,
and all the navies
that were ever built . . .
have not affected the life of man
upon earth
as powerfully as has that
One Solitary Life.

Author unknown

CHECK ONE

The Gospels present Jesus,
not only as risen,
but also
as claiming identity with God —
therefore divinity.

If we accept the Gospels
as being faithful to Jesus' claim,
three options are open to us:

☐ *1 Jesus faked his identity.*

Is it possible that Jesus
faked his identity?
Was he a fraud?
Works like *The Passover Plot*
have seriously explored the possibility.
In the final analysis,
however,
critics and scholars
find such attempts
"fanciful and fascinating," because:

Jesus' teachings,
his utter selflessness,
his keen concern for others —
his respect for the Jewish tradition
his whole life style —
his death —
the events after his death —
these were hardly the
hallmarks of a fraud.

☐ *2 Jesus was deluded about his identity.*

What about the second option?
Is it possible that Jesus
was deluded about who he was?
Was he tragically mistaken
about the most basic
of all things —
his own identity?
The Quest for the Historical Jesus
has seriously probed the possibility.
Here again,
such efforts have been
appraised by scholars,
but also rejected.

How is it possible
that the greatest truths
and insights
ever uttered by man
were spoken by one
who was in tragic error
about the most basic thing
a man can be mistaken about —
his own identity?

☐ 3 *Jesus was who he claimed to be.*

The only remaining option is
that Jesus is God Incarnate.
No one can force another person
to accept this conclusion.
On the other hand,
no person,
if he wants to claim
any intellectual honesty,
can ignore Jesus' claim.

Ultimately,
each and every man
is left with
the awesome mystery
and terrifying freedom
of either accepting
or rejecting Jesus
and what he claimed to be —
the Son of God.

NOT ENOUGH

To know about Christ
is not enough.
To be convinced that
He is the Savior of the world
is not enough.
To affirm your faith in Him
as we do in the Apostles' Creed,
is not enough.

You really don't
actively believe in Christ
until you make a
commitment of your life to Him
and receive Him as your Savior.

Billy Graham, quoted in *Distilled Wisdom*
A. A. Montapert

DON'T STOP HOUNDING ME!

What's wrong with me, Lord?
Why can't I change?
Why do I keep dodging you,
and why do you keep hounding me?
I've tried to forget you, Lord;
but you keep stalking me.
You keep giving me hell inside.
You won't give up on me.
Why?

Maybe that's what love
is all about.
If you can love like that, Lord;
if you can love someone
as stubborn as me,
then you must be God.
And sooner or later,
I'm bound to start loving you.

Lord, don't stop hounding me,
even though it hurts my pride,
deflates my ego,
and sickens my soul.
They say you are all-loving.
Well, you are.
And if that means anything,
it means you care about me.
You have the power to change me,
to reach me, to make me over.

Lord, never give up on me,
even though
I may have all but given up on you.

Now widespread throughout the United States,
the Teen Challenge program
is one of the most successful
drug rehabilitation programs in operation today.

Based on religious experience
and extending over a nine-month period,
the program involves helping the young addict
discover and develop
a deep personal relationship with Jesus.

Anyone interested in how this is done
can read about it in *The Cross and the Switchblade.*
This remarkable paperback
has sold over 4 million copies
and has been made into a movie.
Here are two firsthand accounts
from the book.

"First of all," said John,
"I know this is real.
And you know how?
Because Jesus Christ
seemed to come right out of the Bible.
He became a living person
who wanted to stand with me
through my problems."

"With me,"
said a boy named Joseph,
"he helped me get rid of drugs.
I used goof balls and marijuana,
and I was beginning to skin pop heroin.
I already had the mind habit
and I had to do this thing.
When I heard about Jesus
it kind of shocked me
that he loved people
in spite of all their sins.
It stirred me
when I heard that he
puts real teeth behind his promises,
by coming into us with the baptism
of the Holy Spirit.
The Holy Spirit
is called the Comforter,
they told me.
When I thought of comfort
I thought of a bottle of wine
and a dozen goof balls.
But these guys
were talking about comfort in heaven
where I could feel clean later.

CONVERSION

Early in 1958
a young Pentecostal minister
from Philipsburg Pa.,
felt a call to go to New York City
to help seven boys
from the gang known as "the Dragons,"
who were on trial for the murder
of Michael Farmer.
This was the beginning
of Rev. David Wilkerson's
work among drug addicts,
a work that has resulted in the founding of
the Teen Challenge program.

I got to wanting this . . .
I cried to God for help
and that's when he came around.
He took over my lips
and my tongue
and I was speaking a new language.
At first I thought I was crazy,
but all of a sudden
I knew I couldn't be,
because something was happening too.
I wasn't lonely any more.
I didn't want any more drugs.
I loved everybody.
For the first time in my life
I felt clean."

Commenting on why
Teen Challenge is effective in transforming lives,
one eminent theologian said,

"Teen Challenge is a reminder of biblical doctrines
that are simply missing from
much of contemporary preaching. . . .
One does not hear
any sermons on sin
or conversion or judgment. . . .
These doctrines belong to the biblical message . . .

Teen Challenge is effective
because it preaches the whole biblical message
as the Pentecostals see it,
which includes sin,
conversion,
sanctification,
joy,
peace
and judgment.
This message is simple,
direct
and eminently personal . . .

[Teen Challenge] is effective
because its staff members
have taken seriously
the imitation of Christ
and because they live
Spirit-filled lives.

The Pentecostals and Drug Addiction
Killian McDonnell, *America*

DIFFERENT POWER

Jesus has one
supreme advantage
over all other leaders. . . .
The influence of these [leaders]
on their followers
is purely psychological . . .
That of Jesus on his
is mystical as well . . .

[Great leaders] can stir
the emotions and
sway the passions of men:
They cannot put
their own spirit

or their own force
or their own greatness
into those that
swear loyalty to them.
If these latter are changed,
the change is due to their own
deliberate decisions and actions.

But Jesus can directly
change his adherents. . . .
Grace reinforces
and gives supernatural energy
to the natural psychological influence.

In the Likeness of Christ
Edward Leen

DISCOVERY

Thomas Merton,
tells how he discovered Christ.
It happened one summer
while he was traveling around Europe
on his own.

I don't know how it began—
I found myself looking
into churches . . .

The effect of the discovery
was tremendous . . .
what a thing it
was to come upon . . .
an art that was . . .
urgent in all that it had to say . . .
I began to haunt the churches . . .

And now for the first time in my life
I began to find out something
of who this Person was
that men called Christ. . . .
The saints of those forgotten days
had left upon the walls of their churches
a word
which . . . I was able
in some measure to apprehend. . . .

But above all,
the most real and most immediate source
[of my new knowledge] . . .
was Christ himself,
present in those churches . . .
And it was he
who was teaching me
who he was,
more directly
than I was capable of realizing. . . .

And I bought . . .
the New Testament. . . .
And I read more and more
of the Gospels,
and my love for the old churches
and their mosaics
grew from day to day.
Soon I was no longer visiting them
for art. . . .
something else attracted me:
a kind of interior peace . . .

The Seven Storey Mountain
Thomas Merton

WAKE AND WALK

In my heart
dwells Jesus of Galilee,
the Man above men,
the Poet who
makes poets of us all,
the Spirit who
knocks at our door that
we may wake and rise
and walk out
to meet the truth
naked and unemcumbered.

Jesus The Son of God
Kahlil Gibran
Published by Alfred A. Knopf, Inc.

ALL THE DIFFERENCE

Two roads diverged in a yellow wood,
and sorry I could not travel both
And be one traveler, long I stood
And looked down one as far as I could
To where it bent in the undergrowth;

Then took the other, as just as fair,
And having perhaps a better claim
Because it was grassy and wanted wear . . .

I shall be telling this with a sigh
Somewhere ages and ages hence:
Two roads diverged in a wood, and I —
I took the one less traveled by,
And that has made all the difference.

The Poetry of Robert Frost
Edited by Edward Connery Lathem
Holt, Rinehart and Winston, Inc.

Say to those
who are frightened:
Be strong,
fear not!
Here is our God,
he comes
to save us.

ISAIAH 35:4